COPYRIGHT 2023 COMPUTER NETWORKING FOR BEGINNERS

By Emerito H. Gatchalian

ISBN

Hardbound-978-621-470-894-9

MOBI/KINDLE-978-621-470-895-6

Softbound/Paperback-978-621-470-896-3

Published by:

Poetry Planet Book Publishing House

Rosario, Pozorrubio, Pangasinan, Philippines

Email: maritesritumalta@gmail.com

Contact number: 09300004808

This book is dedicated to my family and everyone who helped me along the way. I haven't expressed my thanks enough and hope you all know in my heart how grateful I am.
– Emerito H. Gatchalian

TABLE OF CONTENTS

ABOUT THE BOOK

COMPUTER NETWORKING FOR BEGINNERS brings you up to speed on fundamental computer concepts and teaches you everything you need to know about networking at the entry-level. This helpful manual, written by a TESDA Computer Systems Servicing (CSS) Certified Trainer and ICT Teacher in Secondary School, takes you step-by-step through the most crucial ideas and abilities you need to be effective in computer networking. Starting from scratch, you'll become familiar with networking concepts, network components, tools, and equipment before moving on to cable configurations and setups. You'll discover how to construct Ethernet cabling, set up patch panels and modular jacks, and arrange cable raceways. You are guided through Network Safety Precautions by clear instructions. You'll even learn how to design your network and choose among the types of networks most appropriate to your organization. Perhaps you're brushing up for a new IT job, getting ready for a computer course, or simply wondering how a computer network might make your life easier. If networking is completely new to you, this is your comprehensive guide to mastering the necessary skills:

1. Fundamental Computer Network Concepts
2. Network Technology
3. Network Topology
4. Network Materials, Tools, and Devices
5. Transmission Media
6. Ethernet Cable Configurations
7. Cable Management
8. Raceway in Cabling System
9. Network Safety Precautions

COMPUTER NETWORKING FOR BEGINNERS will have you up and running quickly with its clear explanations and step-by-step guidance.

ABOUT THE AUTHOR

Emerito Hernandez Gatchalian is a Senior High School ICT Teacher at Balagtas National Agricultural High School (BNAHS). He previously had positions as systems administrator and computer programmer in different companies in Manila and abroad. He also previously worked as a College Instructor at a prestigious computer school in Manila. He lives in the City of Malolos with his wife and three children. He is now completing his master's degree in information technology. He enjoys exploring new places, going on trips, and trying new things.

INTRODUCTION

Welcome to *Computer Networking For Beginners*! This book contains sets of chapters that focus on a variety of fundamental topics about computer networking. Chapters are arranged in a way that allows even the completely first-time learners in computer to effortlessly take in the various networking concepts. Just as it is the norm to start with basics, the book sets out with an introduction that allows you to grasp the meaning of computer networks. Given the fact that the book introduces you to the fundamentals of networking, it certainly come out sufficiently equipped with a good deal of knowledge to understand the current network technology. As you move further down, subsequent chapters offer more advanced networking concepts such as network topologies and cabling management. Most importantly, the book talks about different types of network architectures and their configurations.

This book's rigorous research and organization, together with its clarity and conciseness, make it easy for you to quickly learn the extremely valuable networking skills you need to get started on the path to a rewarding networking career. I am confident that knowledge will emerge from the book with the necessary know-how to get you started in this subject given the practical approach it takes

CHAPTER 1

FUNDAMENTAL COMPUTER NETWORK CONCEPTS

In this chapter, you will begin by understanding the process of data communication. Once you have a basic understanding of how we communicate and share information, it will be easier to understand the concept of computer networks. After going through this chapter, you are expected to:

1. understand the principle of data communication in a network;
2. demonstrate understanding of the fundamental concepts of computer network;
3. discuss, differentiate, and elaborate the different types of networks; and
4. appreciate the functions of computer networks.

Networks seem to be everywhere. There is not anything you can do with data these days that does not require the use of a network. Computer networks, like human networks, enable us to share data and resources. The use of networks in industry is much more widespread than it is in homes and schools. Individuals and companies alike benefit from networks, which not only help them save money but also generate revenue.

Data Communication & Computer Network

When we communicate, we share information. This sharing can be local or remote. Communication between individuals and local communication usually occurs face to face, while remote communication takes place over distance (see Figure 1.1).

Figure 1.1 Type of Communications

Data communication refers to the transmission of digital data between two or more computers connected to a computer network. It involves cables and wires, but others are sent wirelessly. There are five (5) components of data communications namely, message, sender, receiver, transmission medium and protocol. Figure 1.2 shows how these components interact with each other when sender transmit message to receiver using a transmission medium.

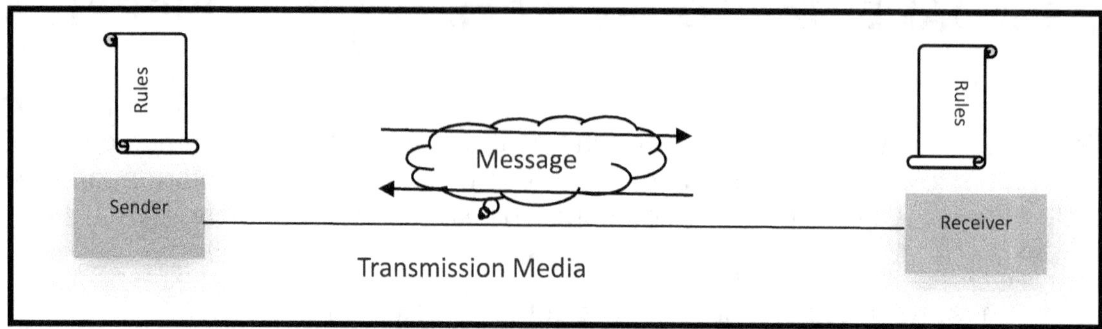

Figure 1.2 Components of Data Communications

1. **Message**. The message is the information (data) to be communicated. Popular forms of information include text, numbers, pictures, audio, and video.
2. **Sender**. The sender is the device that sends the data message. It can be a computer, workstation, telephone handset, video camera, and so on.
3. **Receiver**. The receiver is the device that receives the message. It can be a computer, workstation, telephone handset, television, and so on.
4. **Transmission medium.** The transmission medium is the physical path by which a message travels from sender to receiver. Some examples of transmission media include twisted-pair wire, coaxial cable, fiber-optic cable, and radio waves.
5. **Protocol.** A protocol is a set of rules that govern data communications. It represents an agreement between the communication devices. Without a protocol, two devices may be connected but not communicating, just as a person speaking French cannot be understood by a person who speaks only Japanese.

What is a computer network?

A computer network is a group of computers and other computing devices (a phone, laptop, printer, or a personal organizer) that are linked together through communication devices so that they can share information and resources (refer to Figure 1.3). **Communication devices** refer to any type of hardware capable of transmitting data, instructions, and information between a sending device and a receiving device. Examples of these devices are Bluetooth, infrared, modem, smartphone, WIFI and other devices used to transmit data. These communication devices use transmission media to communicate with each other.

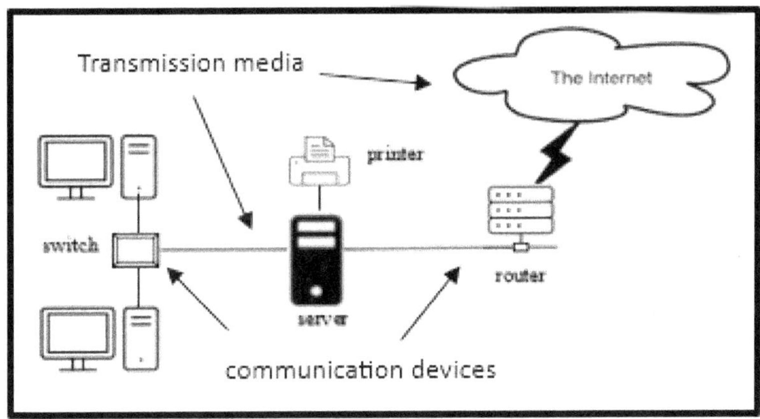

Figure 1.3 Computer network links

There are two types of transmission media namely, **Guided transmission media** and **Unguided transmission media**. Figure 1.4 shows the category of transmission media.

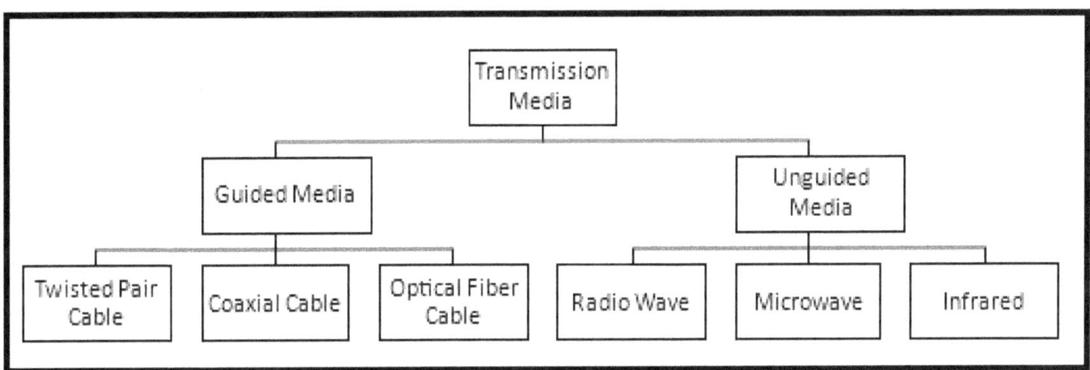

Figure 1.4 Category of Transmission Media

Guided transmission media are also called bounded media or wired media. They comprise cables or wires through which data is transmitted. The most popular are twisted pair cable, coaxial cable, and optical fiber cable.

Unguided transmission media are also called wireless media. They transport data in the form of electromagnetic waves that do not require any cables for transmission. These types of communication are commonly referred to as wireless communications. The most used unguided transmission media are radio wave, microwave, and infrared.

What Networks Do?

Computer networks are used to carry out many tasks through the sharing of information. Some of the things that networks are used include:

1. Communicating using email, video, instant messaging, social media etc.
2. Sharing devices such as printers, scanners, and photocopiers
3. Sharing files
4. Sharing software and operating programs on remote systems
5. Allowing network users to easily access and maintain information.

Types of Computer Networks

A computer network can be categorized by its size into four types:

o   Local Area Network (LAN)

o   Personal Area Network (PAN)

o   Metropolitan Area Network (MAN)

o   Wide Area Network (WAN)

Local Area Network (LAN)

This network refers to a group of computers connected to each other in a small area such as a building, school, or office. They are used for connecting two or more computers through a transmission medium such as twisted pair and coaxial cable. It is less costly as it is built with inexpensive hardware such as hubs, network adapters, and ethernet cables. The data is transferred at an extremely fast rate in the Local Area Network. In terms of security, LAN provides higher security. Figure 1.5 shows the Local Area Network with network devices such as computers, hub, and printer.

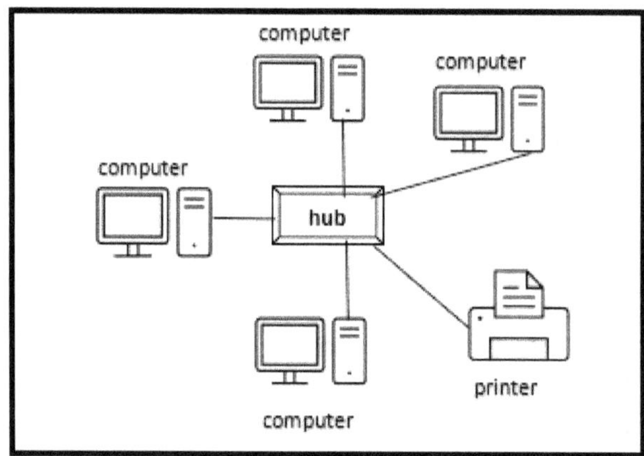

Figure 1.5 Local Area Network

Personal Area Network (PAN)

This network is arranged within an individual person's workplace, typically within a range of 10 meters (see Figure 1.6). Personal Area Network is used for connecting the computer to different devices of personal use. Personal devices that are used to develop this network are the personal computer, laptop, mobile phones, media player and play stations. This network is inexpensive, secure, and reliable but can only be used in short range and the transfer of data is slow.

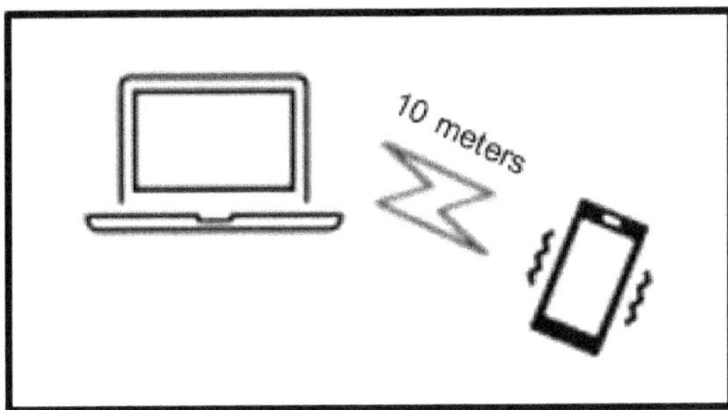

Figure 1.6 Personal Area Network

There are two (2) types of PAN namely, *Wired Personal Area Network* and *Wireless Personal Area Network.*

Wireless Personal Area Network uses wireless technologies such as Wi-Fi and Bluetooth. It is considered a low range network. **Wired Personal Area Network** provides short connections between peripherals such as Universal Serial Bus (USB), printer and external hard drives.

Metropolitan Area Network (MAN)

This network refers to a network that covers a large geographic area by interconnecting multiple LANs to form a larger network. Usually, the government agencies use MAN to connect to the citizens and private industries through a telephone exchange line within a metropolitan area, multiple cities and towns, or any given large area with multiple buildings (refer to Figure 1.7).

This network is less expensive than the Wide Area Network (WAN) and gives better efficiency and easily managed data. Unlike WAN, this network provides a highly-security level and centralized administration of the system's resources.

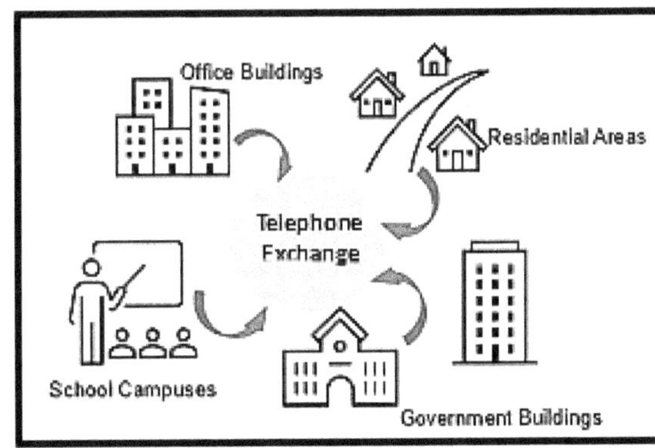

Figure 1.7 Metropolitan Area Network

Wide Area Network (WAN)

This network extends over large geographical areas such as cities, provinces, or countries. It spans over a large geographical area through a telephone line, fiber optic cable or satellite links. The internet is one of the biggest WANs in the world. Wide Area Network is widely used in the field of business, government, and education (see Figure 1.8).

The main advantage of WAN is that it spans over a very large geographical area and connects a huge mass of people. But setting up WAN costs more money because it involves purchasing expensive equipment such as servers, routers, switches, and extra security software. WAN has more security problems as compared to other types of networks. It involves many technologies combined with each other which can create a security gap if not managed effectively.

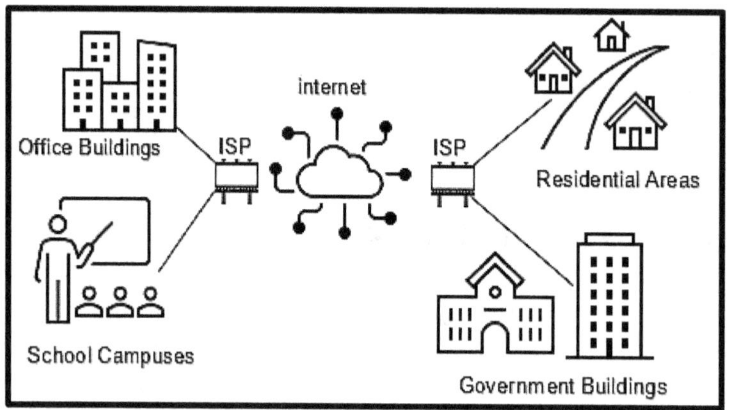

Figure 1.8 Wide Area Network

Computer networks allow computers to connect and communicate with different computers via any medium. PAN, LAN, MAN, and WAN are the four major types of the network designed to operate over the area they cover. There are some similarities and dissimilarities between them. The table below shows their major differences in the geographical area they cover, error rates, transmission speed and networking cost.

Category	PAN	LAN	MAN	WAN
Area Covered	Up to 10 Meter radius	Up to 10-Kilometer radius	Up to 100 Kilometer radius	No boundary
Error Rates	Very minimal	Very minimal	Minimal	Very High
Transmission Speed	Very High	Very High	Moderate	Slow
Networking Cost	Minimal	Moderate	Expensive	Highly Expensive

Table 1.1 Comparison of PAN, LAN, MAN, WAN

CHAPTER 2

NETWORK TECHNOLOGY

In this chapter, you will understand the concept of network architecture and communication technology. Once you understand the concept of network architecture, the prevailing communication technology, and their importance in strategic planning, it will be easier to decide which technology is applicable to your organization. After going through this chapter, you are expected to:

1. define network architecture and its types;
2. discuss, differentiate, and elaborate the difference between Peer-to-Peer and Client-Server architecture;
3. demonstrate understanding of network communication technology;
4. identify and differentiate the different types of network communication technology and appreciate the benefits of network technology.

In this consistently advancing world of interconnected activities, it has never been more essential to consider network design when growing new circumstances into the bigger undertaking organization. Managers need information readily available to settle on choices immediately, yet occasionally they ought to forget the security of the organization conveying that information. The objective of a computing network is to bring together information while keeping the basic structure isolated in a manner that empowers protection inside and out. There ought to be an appropriate organizational system plan.

Before there can be a proper network design, the first step that needs to be taken is network architecture analysis. You cannot go into network design without first knowing what is needed, hence the analysis stage of network setup.

Network Technology

It involves the use of technology to the management and distribution of digital resources via a computer network through the transmission of data using communication media like cables, wires, router, and other wireless media. This technology enables data exchange between two or more networks for the benefit of mutual traffic exchange. It controls how our organization uses the network and accesses its resources. Therefore, it is crucial to carefully plan how we create our network infrastructure. With the proper network design, your company can continue to be connected while also getting dependable network speeds.

Network Architecture

It is a design structure for the physical components of a network, as well as their functional arrangement and configuration, as well as the network's operating concepts and procedures and communication protocols.

Network architecture is also known as network model or network design. It describes the design of the computer network that defines how a computer network is configured and what strategies are being used. It is mainly focusing on the function of the networks.

It includes assessing and seeing how every one of the components of the network connect (from switches, switches, and workers to work areas, PCs, and printers) and how they can be made to run as effectively as could really be expected. A very much planned network can bring expanded operational efficiency.

There are several ways in which a computer network can be designed. The network architecture states how computers are organized in a system and how tasks are allocated between these computers.

There are two (2) widely used types of network architecture; (1) *peer-to-peer network* and (2) *client-server network.*

Both peer-to-peer and client-server networks connect computers so that resources like files and applications can be shared by its members within the network. *Peer-to-peer* networks link computers together so that they can share all or part of their resources. *Client-server* networks have one or more central computers, called servers, that store the data and control resources. Client/server architecture is also called 'tiered' because it uses multiple levels.

Peer-To-Peer Network (P2P)

Peer-to-peer is mostly used for resource sharing. As shown in Figure 2.1, it involves each computer connected to the network through a hub sharing resources such as files, applications, disk drives, DVD players and printers with other computers on the network. Every computer on the network has access to these common resources anytime. Each computer serves as both a client and a server, communicating with other computers directly. A printer on one computer, for example, may be used by any other computer on a peer-to-peer network.

There is no real hierarchy among computers, and all of them are considered equal. This is referred to as a distributed architecture or workgroup.

The main advantage of this network is inexpensive to set up. All you need is a way to connect computers using Ethernet cable, hub, or a Wi-Fi router.

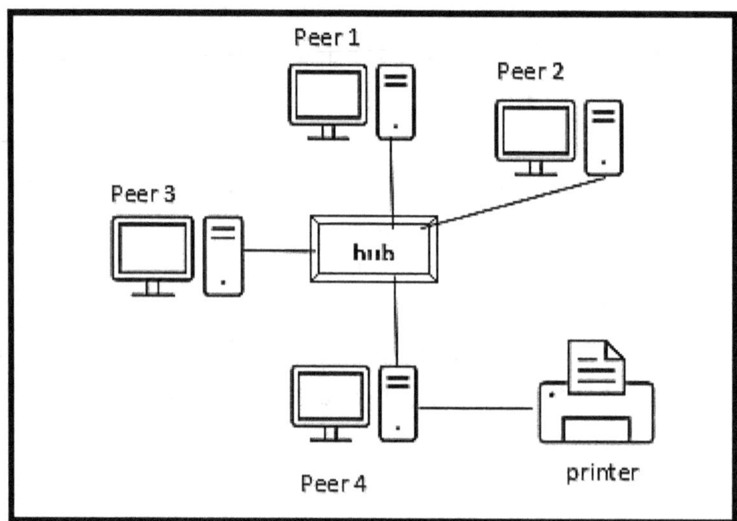

Figure 2.1 Peer to Peer Network

Advantages of Peer-to-peer Network
1. No need to install a network operating system.
2. Does not need an expensive server because individual workstations are used to store and access the files.
3. No need for network administrator because each user sets their own permissions as to which resources, they are willing to share.
4. Much easier to set up than a client-server network - does not need advanced knowledge in networking.
5. If one computer fails, it will not affect any other part of the network.

Disadvantages of Peer-to-peer Network
1. There will be an effect on performance when a computer is being accessed by others.
2. Files and folders cannot be centrally backed up.
3. There might be scattered files because they are not centrally organized into a specific 'shared area'.

4. The possibility of virus attack because installation of antivirus software is the responsibility of each individual user.
5. There is little or no security besides the permissions. Users are not required to log onto their workstations.

Client-Server Network

A client-server network involves multiple clients, or *workstations*, connecting to at least one central server (refer to Figure 2.2). Most applications and files are installed on the server. When a client needs any of these resources, it needs to access them from the server. Server who keeps records of user's rights, check the validity of the request. If the requesting client has the right to access, the request is granted, otherwise an error message will be displayed. Clients-server networks have faster access speeds because of the large number of clients they are designed to support. The clients are allowed to function as workstations without sharing any of their own resources. It is easier to upgrade software applications on a client-server network because files are held on one single computer. Security is also high on a client server network because the security is handled by the server alone.

With a client server network, files will not be stored on the hard drive of each computer, instead they will be stored on a high-end computer called a *server*. A server is intended to efficiently provide data to remote clients.

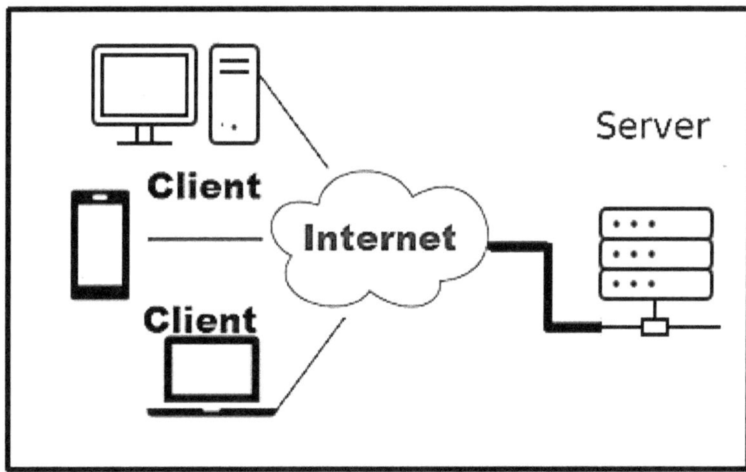

Figure 2.2 Client/Server Network

 Remember:

Client is a computer that needs service and only the server can serve that request.

Server is a computer that provides services to clients and manages their access to hardware, software, and other resources of the network.

Advantages of Client-Server
1. Centralized control. All the necessary information is placed in a single location.
2. The data is well protected due to its centralized architecture that can enforce access controls such that only authorized users are granted access.
3. It is highly scalable. Increasing the size of the clients and servers will not cause many interruptions.
4. It has the best management to track and find records of required files.
5. Every client is provided with the opportunity to log into the system regardless of location and platform.

Disadvantages of Client Server Network
1. The primary disadvantage of client-server network is the congestion of the network. If too many clients make requests from the same server at the same time, it will result in crashes or slowing down of the connection.
2. In case the main server fails, then the whole network will be disrupted.
3. The set-up cost and maintenance are usually high.
4. Too server-oriented which makes the dedicated server work non-stop.
5. Requires a network administrator to manage the system.

Communication Technology

It involves the use of technology by an organization to support internal and external communication and collaboration. There are three (3) types of communication technology implemented by different organizations to transmit data namely intranet, extranet and the internet.

Intranet

An intranet is a private network within an organization that resembles the internet. It is a constrained version of the internet that provides more security in its network (refer to Figure 2.3). It is used by the company to secure a network that can only be accessed by that company's employees. This intranet serves as the portal for employees to access internal and external resources, and enables workers to communicate, collaborate, and share documents and other information. Typical applications include electronic phone directory, email addresses, employee information, internal job openings and others.

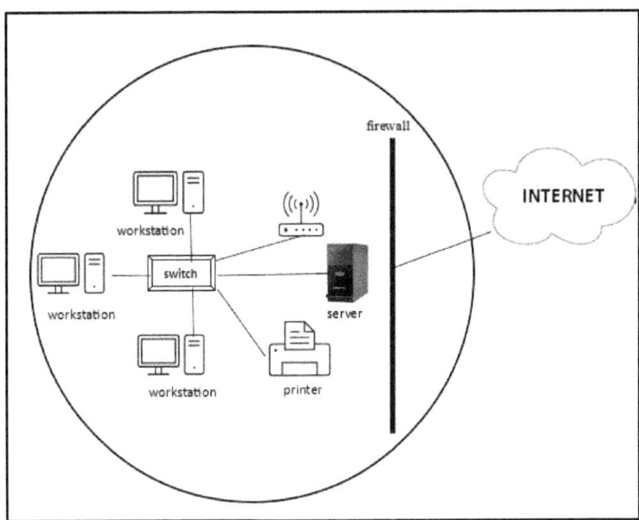

Figure 2.3 Intranet

Benefits of Intranet
1. **Improves internal communication**. Intranet helps companies increase internal communication. Staff can share ideas, have open dialogues, and management can quickly keep employees up to date, among other things.
2. **Assists Employee in locating information.** The intranet allows for the rapid broadcast of critical information. Employees may acquire the most up-to-date information regarding meetings, seminars, and team-building events, among other things, thanks to the platform's simple navigation.
3. **Management of data and documents**. An intranet manages company's data with pinpoint accuracy. Employees can access information on the dashboard in real time. The intranet prevents information overlap, allowing employees to focus on what they need. The document management system, mostly on intranet, makes the filling system easier by tagging your files.
4. **Process consolidation**. An intranet eliminates the need for multiple pieces of software to do accounting, HR, and marketing duties. It unifies them into a single system, resulting in increased productivity and profit margins.
5. **It strengthens your brand and values**. It gives a variety of options for expressing the company's ideals. This is accomplished by rewarding employees who embody the company's values, facilitating the sharing of relevant web articles that support the company's values, and allowing employees to express some of the values they experience at work.

Extranet

A private network that connects more than one organization. Extranet is typically use some kind of virtual private network (VPN) connection or via the internet with additional authentication measures to allow suppliers, customers and business partners limited access to an organization's network (refer to Figure 2.4). The purpose is to increase efficiency and reduce costs. It is the type of network that allows users from outside to access the Intranet of an organization.

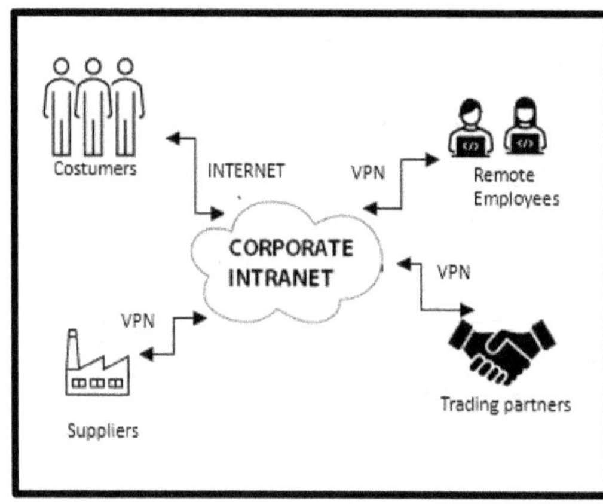

Figure 2.4 Extranet

Benefits of Extranet

1. **Improve your ability to communicate and collaborate**. Extranet allows effective communication and collaboration with clients, customers, and stakeholders via a secure network.
2. **Consolidation of supply chains**. Using extranet, the consolidation processes will be easy such as online ordering, order tracking and inventory management.
3. **Reduce costs.** Manuals and technical documentation are available online to trading partners and customers.
4. **Enhance your business relationships**. Because of the close collaborative working that extranets support, there will be an improved business relationship between the company and its clients, suppliers, and business partners.
5. **Improve customer service** – Allowing the customers direct access to information and enabling them to resolve their own queries will improve customer service.
6. **Simplify processes**. Using a single user interface between the company and its stakeholders will simplify processes.
7. **Secured and reliable communications**. Extranet allows the exchanges to take place in a controlled, secure, and reliable environment.
8. **Share exclusive information** – Allowing sharing of product development information exclusively with partner companies.
9. **Flexible working time**. Remote and mobile employees may access critical business information 24 hours a day, no matter where they are.

Internet

The internet is a public network that can be accessed by anyone, anytime and anywhere through ISPs. The Internet, sometimes called simply "the Net," is a worldwide system of computer networks -- a network of networks. It connects computer systems across the world in high-bandwidth communication lines that comprise the Internet "backbone." These lines are connected to major Internet hubs that distribute data to your ISPs and Web servers as shown in Figure 2.5.

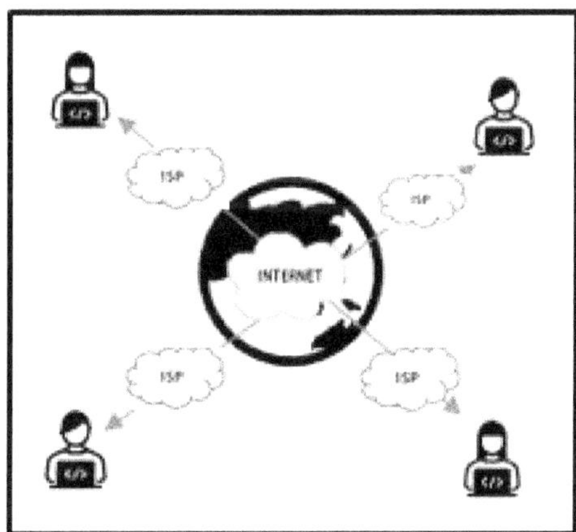

Figure 2.5 The Internet

Benefits of Internet
1. The Internet is a medium that connects people around the world allowing them to share information and communicate anytime and anywhere.
2. E-commerce
3. Online-education
4. Online Games, Entertainment and Lifestyle
5. Access to resources and instant information

Table 2.1 shows the point of difference between the three (3) types of communication technology in terms of accessibility of network, availability, coverage, accessibility of content, number of computers connected , owner, purpose of the network, security, users and economical.

Point of Difference	Internet	Intranet	Extranet
Accessibility of network	Public	Private	Private
Availability	Worldwide system.	Specific to an organization.	Sharing information with customers and trading partners makes the use of a public network.
Coverage	All over the world.	Restricted area up to an organization.	Restriction based on policies set by the organization and its stakeholders.
Accessibility of content	Global access	It is accessible only to the members of the organization.	Accessible only to the members of the organization and external members with security
No. of computers connected	Unlimited numbers of devices	Minimal number of devices	Minimal number of devices
Owner	No one.	Single organization.	Single/ Multiple organizations.
Purpose of the network	Its purpose is to share information to anyone	Its purpose is to share information to the members of the organization	Its purpose is to share information between internal and external stakeholders.
Security	Dependent on the security set by the users on their machines.	It is enforced via firewall.	It is enforced via a firewall that separates internet and extranet.
Users	Anyone	Employees of the organization.	Employees of the organization and the member stakeholders
Economical	Very economical	Less economical.	Less economical.

Table 2.1 Difference between Internet, Intranet and Extranet

CHAPTER 3

NETWORK TOPOLOGY

In this module, you will understand the concept of network topology which is very important to understand the different elements of our network and what we can expect from their performance. Your basic understanding of network topology will help you in designing your computer networks. After going through this chapter, you are expected to:

1. define network topology and its types;
2. discuss, differentiate, and elaborate the difference between the types of network topology;
3. demonstrate understanding of how the different network topologies are connected; and
4. perform an analysis on the different factors to be considered in choosing network topology.

If you would like to understand the importance of networking concepts, the topology will help you understand the physical and logical aspects of the network. Without understanding the network topology, we will not understand how computer networks work.

Topology stands as a significant element of network design theory. The layout of a network has a substantial impact on its functionality. Selecting the right topology will increase performance and data efficiency, as well as optimize resource allocation and lower operating costs.

Network Topology

It is the physical and logical arrangement of the elements (called nodes) of a network. It shows how computers and devices in networks link to each other. It also shows how data transmission happens between these nodes. Generally, it denotes the interrelated model of network components.

There are five basic physical network topologies as shown in Figure 3.1 namely star, ring, bush, tree, and mesh. But networks usually use combinations of these topologies - called Hybrid.

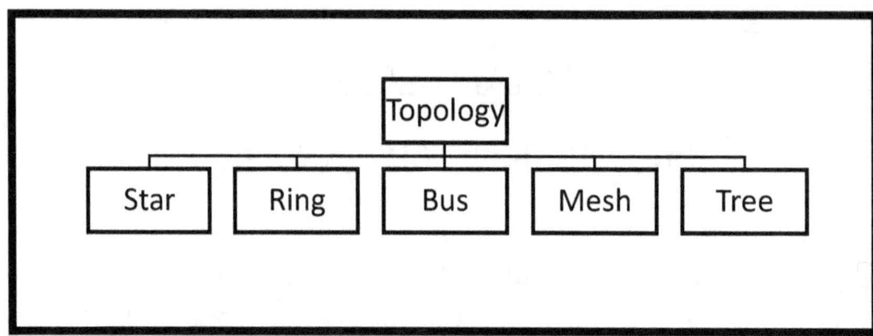

Figure 3.1 Basic Physical Network Topologies

Bus Topology

In bus topology, a single long cable serves as a backbone connecting all the devices in a network. At each end, a terminator is linked to stop signals from bouncing back along the cable. Since the signal travels along the cable and weakens as it goes along the route, the bus topology can only accommodate a small number of devices. Figure 3.1 shows the diagram of Bus Topology.

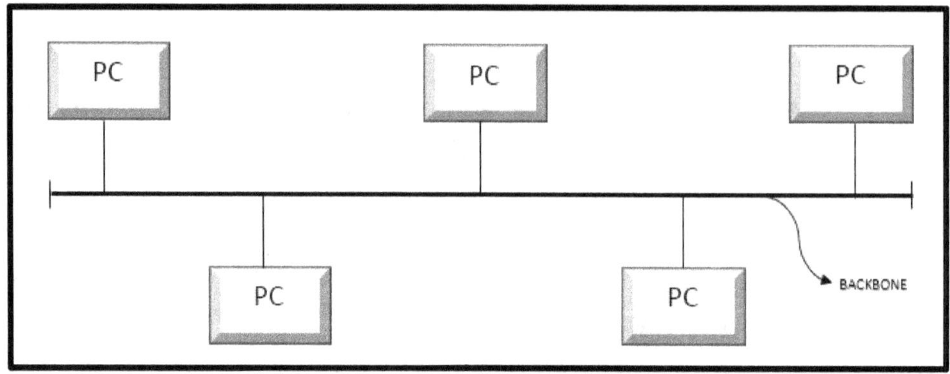

Figure 3.1 Bus Topology

How is Bus Topology Connected?
Figure 3.2 shows the Bus Topology with coaxial cable and BNC connectors. It has single cable (coaxial) functions as the shared communication medium for all the devices attached with this cable with interface connectors. There are two types of BNC connectors. These are the male and female connectors as shown in Figure 3.3.

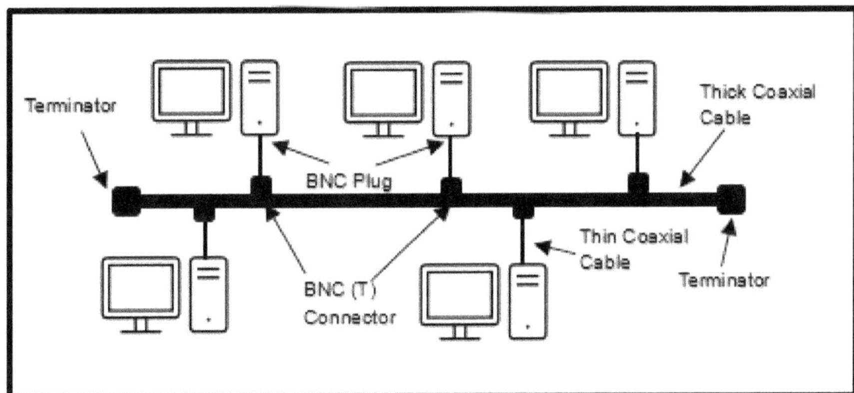

Figure 3.2 Bus Topology with Coaxial Cable and BNC Connector

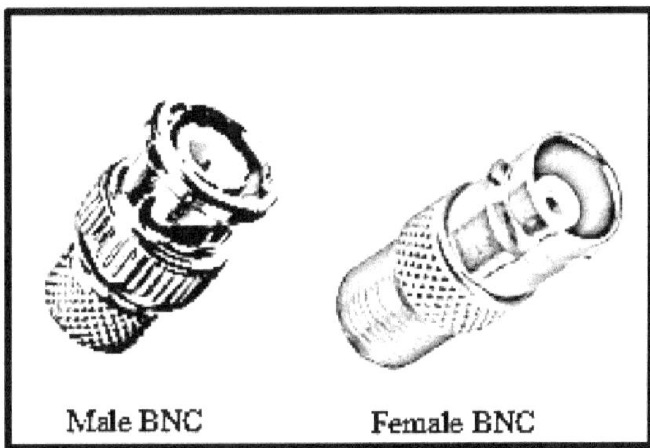

Figure 3.3 BNC Connectors

Advantages of Bus Topology
- ✓ It is easy to set up.
- ✓ It is cost-effective because it uses less cabling than other topologies.
- ✓ If needed, more nodes can be easily added to the network by joining additional cables.

Disadvantages of Bus Topology
- ✓ It is difficult to find the problem if some fault occurs in the network.
- ✓ The entire network malfunctions if there is a failure in the main cable.
- ✓ data is "half-duplex," which means it can't be sent in two opposite directions at the same time. This layout is not the ideal choice for networks with huge amounts of traffic.

Ring Topology

In ring topology, each device/host is connected to two neighboring devices on either side of it. A signal is passed along the ring in one direction, from device to device, until it reaches its destination. Each device in the ring incorporates a repeater that pass signal to the next device.

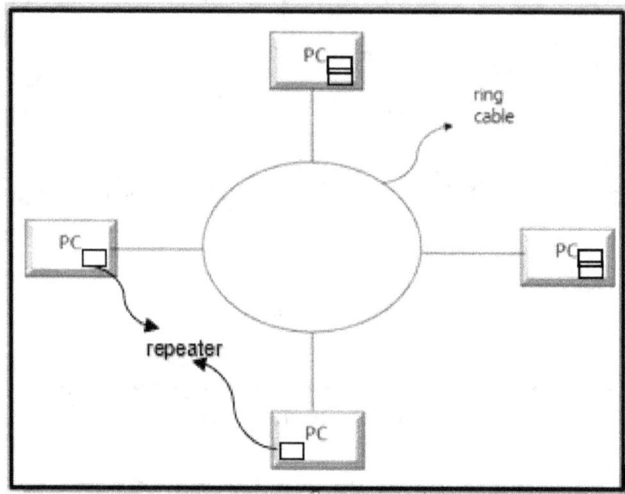

Figure 3.4 Ring Topology with Repeater

How is Ring Topology Connected?

Depending on the network card used in each computer of the ring topology, a coaxial cable (act as ring cable) or an RJ-45 network cable is used to connect computers together. Figure 3.5 shows a network card used to setup ring topology.

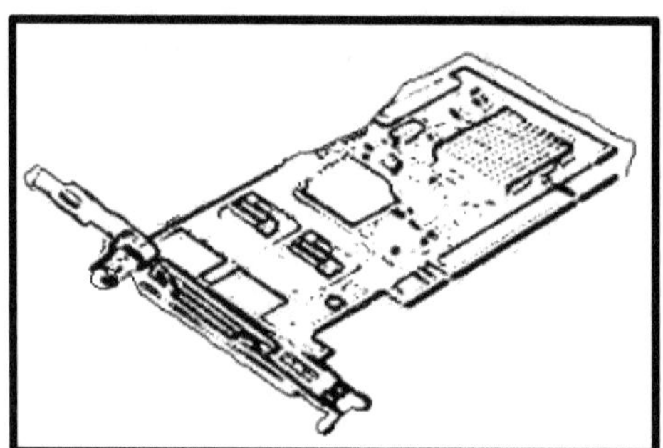

Figure 3.5 Ring Topology Network Card

Advantages of Ring Topology
- ✓ It is relatively simple to set up and customize.
- ✓ Relatively easy to manage and identify issues on the network.
- ✓ No data collision

Disadvantages of Ring Topology
- ✓ A connection failure will bring the entire network down.
- ✓ Adding a new device to the network requires shutting down the entire network.
- ✓ Since all the data is circulating in a loop, there are traffic problems.

Star Topology

Each device in star topology is connected to a central controller known as the hub or switch (refer to Figure 3.6). These devices are not in direct communication with one another. The hub serves as a central server, allowing one device to send data to another by sending it to the hub, which then relays it to the other connected device. In most cases, a high-speed LAN employs a star topology.

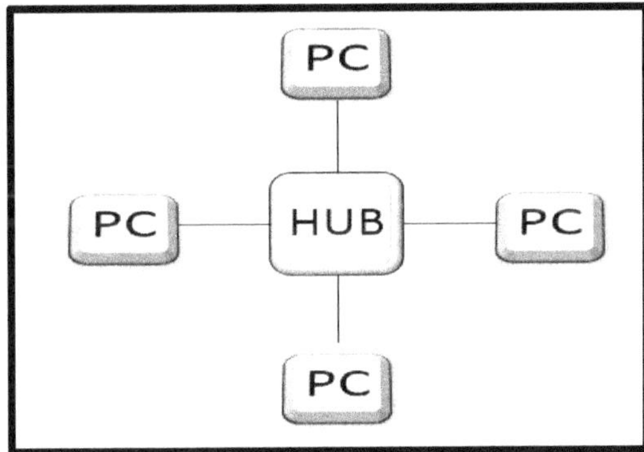

Figure 3.6 Star Topology with Hub

How is Star Topology Connected?

In star topology a networking switch or a hub is used as the centralized device. Each computer in the network is using a separate twisted pair cable to connect to the switch. Twisted pair cable uses RJ-45 connectors on both ends.

Advantages of Star Topology

✓ Since each device only requires one I/O port to connect to the hub, it is less costly.
✓ It is easy to set up and configure.
✓ It is stable, meaning that if one connection fails, the other links are unaffected.
✓ It is easy to find problems in this topology.

Disadvantages of Star Topology

✓ This topology is too dependent on the hub. If the hub fails, the whole network goes down with it.
✓ More cabling is required since each node must be linked to the central hub.

Mesh Topology

Every device in a mesh topology has its own dedicated point-to-point connection to every other device as shown in Figure 3.7. Each device on the network is linked to any other device on the network through a separate connection, making it resilient and preventing traffic congestion.

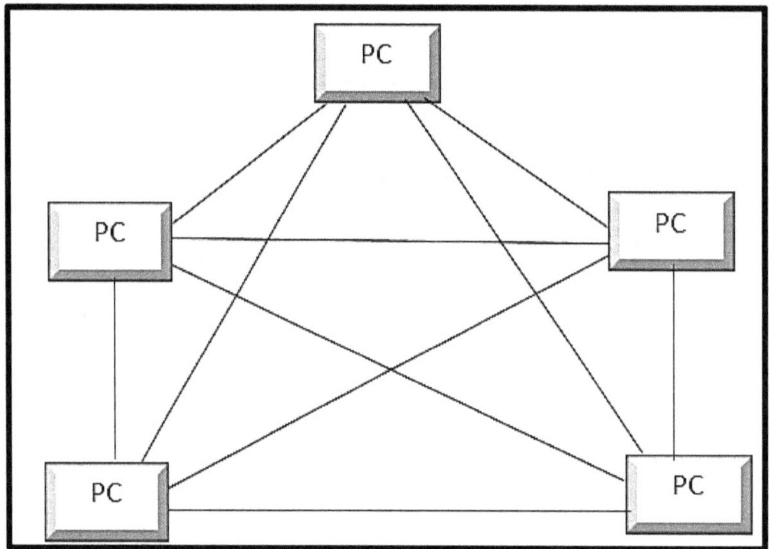

Figure 3.7 Mesh Topology

How is Mesh Topology Connected?

A mesh network is a network topology in which infrastructure nodes (such as bridges, switches, and other infrastructure devices) link directly, dynamically, and non-hierarchically to as many other nodes as possible and collaborate to route data from/to clients as efficiently as possible.

Figure 3.8 shows that mesh is implemented wirelessly which comprises various wireless nodes with access points (usually a router). Each node in the network acts as a forwarding node to transfer the data. Since the network is decentralized, forwarding of data is possible only to the neighboring node. This results in the network structure being simple and easy.

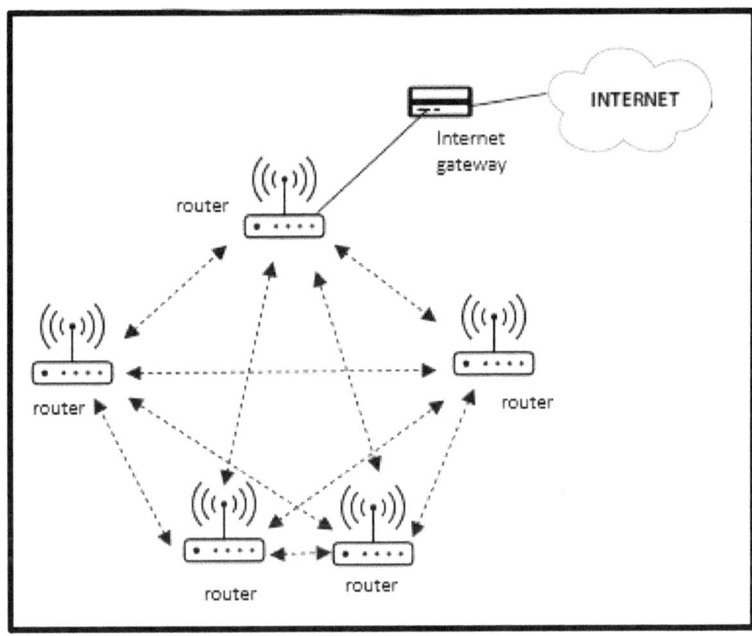

Figure 3.8 Wireless implementation of Mesh Topology

Advantages of Mesh Topology

✓ It is robust since each system is linked to other devices through a dedicated connection, which eliminates traffic congestion that can arise when several devices share links.
✓ It is more secure.
✓ Data transmission between devices is not disrupted by adding more devices.
✓ A failure of one device does not disrupt the network.
✓ Adding additional devices does not disrupt data transmission between other devices.

Disadvantages of Mesh Topology

✓ Higher cost of implementing the network because there is many cablings and the number of I/O ports required.
✓ Building and maintaining the network is difficult.

Tree Topology

The bus and star topologies are combined in tree topology as shown in Figure 3.8. A tree topology is made up of groups of star topologies that are linked by a bus that serves as a backbone cable. Tree Topology is used to extend an existing network.

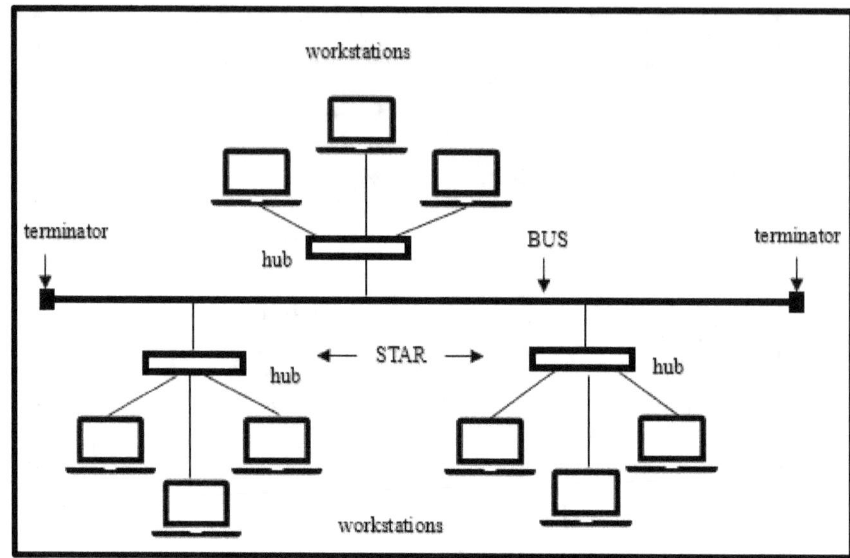

Figure 3.8 Tree Topology

How is Tree Topology Connected?

Since tree topology consists of bus and star topology, it uses two types of connection to the network. All devices in star topology are connected to its central hub/switch. Then, this star topology network connects to bus topology using a backbone hub/switch as shown in Figure 3.9.

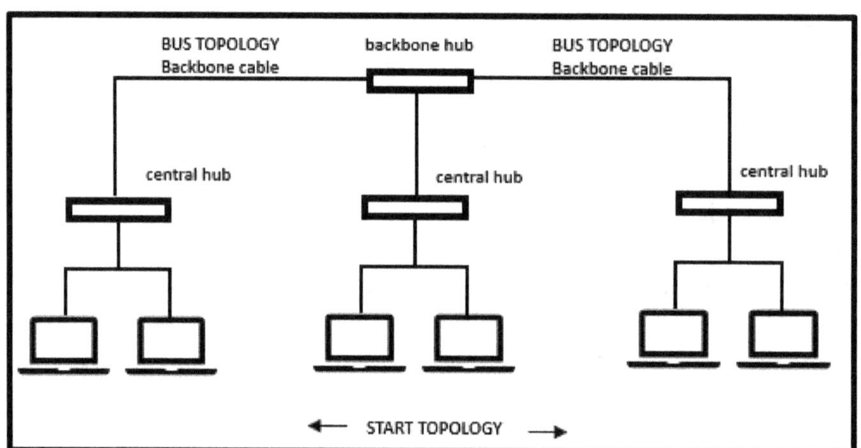

Figure 3.9 Tree Topology with Backbone Hub

Advantages of Tree Topology

✓ It is a combination of easy to set-up topologies - bus and star.
✓ It provides high scalability because you can easily add more nodes.
✓ If one of the computers failed, the other computers are not affected,
✓ It provides easy maintenance and failure identification.

Disadvantages of Tree Topology

✓ More cabling is required as compared to other topologies.
✓ Once the hub fails, the entire network is affected.
✓ Difficult to configure than other network topologies.

Hybrid Topology

A hybrid topology uses two or more different network topologies as shown in Figure 3.10. This topology can include a mix of bus topology, mesh topology, ring topology, star topology, and tree topology.

The decision to use a hybrid topology over a regular topology is based on the organization's need. The decision is influenced by many technical factors like the number of computers, their location, budget, and the desired network functionalities.

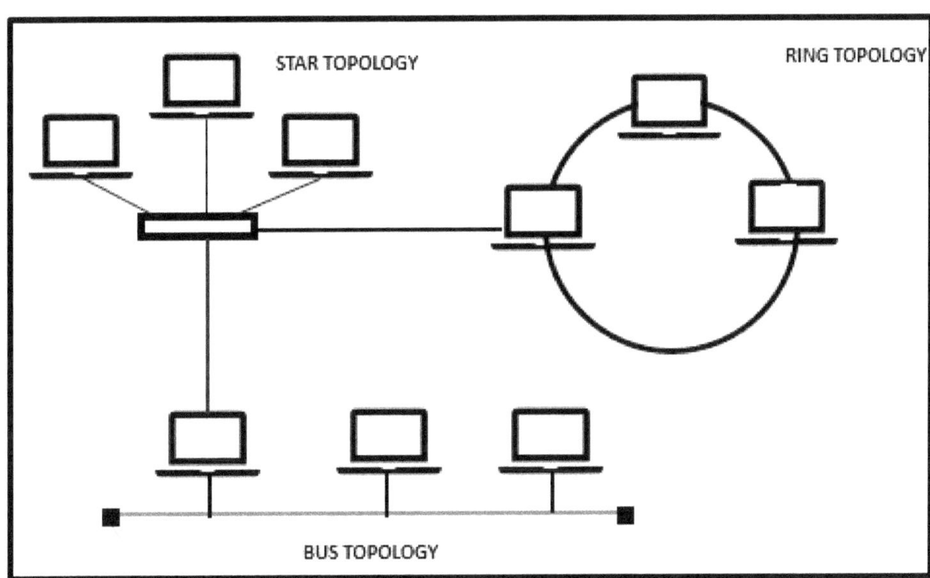

Figure 3.10 Hybrid Topology

Advantages of Hybrid Topology
✓ Can be modified as per requirement.
✓ It is very flexible.
✓ It is very reliable.
✓ Easy integration of new hardware components.
✓ Easy error detecting and troubleshooting.
✓ Handles a large volume of traffic.

Disadvantage of Hybrid Topology
- ✓ Very costly network
- ✓ The design is very complex, and the installation is difficult.
- ✓ There are hardware compatibility issues.
- ✓ Maintenance cost is high.

Considerations When Choosing a Network Topology

When it comes to network topology, there is no such thing as a one-size-fits-all solution. In one company, what is ideal can be insufficient in another. The following are the most important considerations when choosing a network topology.

- **Budget**. A linear bus network may be the least expensive way to install a network; you do not have to purchase hubs or switches.
- **Hardware Resources**. Perform an inventory of your current hardware. You may already have the hardware needed to implement a certain type of topology. So instead of buying everything, your existing resources give you a head start.
- **Ease of Implementation**. The complexity of the network topology you choose is an issue if you are novice in network implementation. In that case, the bus and star topologies are simpler. The mesh, tree and hybrid, on the other hand, are complex and difficult.
- **Size of Network**. Consider the total number of devices to be interconnected. The tree topology works well with large networks. The bus topology is best suited for small organizations.
- **Reliability**. Network topologies aren't always made equal when it comes to reliability. Under heavy loads, ring topology performs admirably, but it is vulnerable to a single point of failure. The star topology is independent of any node, but if the center fails, the network will collapse. On the durability front, mesh and hybrid topologies come out on top.
- **Future growth**. If you are expecting the organization to expand its network, choose a network topology that is readily scalable. With a star topology, expanding a network is easily done by adding another concentrator. But the tree topology is perhaps the most compatible with future expansion requirements as it's easy to extend or shrink the network.

CHAPTER 4

NETWORK MATERIALS, TOOLS, AND DEVICES

In this module, you will be familiarizing yourself with networking materials, tools, and devices. Once you have understood their uses, functionalities, and advantages, it will help you to manage your network project and build it faster and easier. Having the right materials, tools and devices also keeps your network running at optimum performance. After going through this chapter, you are expected to:

1. identify the different network materials, tools, and devices;
2. demonstrate understanding of how these network materials., tools and devices are used in building computer network;
3. enumerate the uses and functions of different network materials, tools, and devices; and
4. understand the value of properly use of materials, tools, and devices in building computer network;

Network materials, tools and devices are needed in building computer networks to provide connectivity and functionality. Understanding how these networking tools and devices work, familiarizing how these network materials can be utilized, and recognizing the roles they played in building computer networks are necessary skills for any computer professional. This module discusses popular networking materials, tools, and devices, and while you are unlikely to use them, you will learn about them.

Network Materials

Network materials are the supplies needed for building computer networks including accessories, furniture, racks, cables, connectors, plugs etc.

The availability of materials of suitable quality and quantity is a basic factor in making decisions on the building of a computer network, regardless of the size and scope. Some of the important materials in implementing computer networks are the following:

1. **Networking cables**. These materials are used to connect one network device to other network devices or to connect two or more computers to share printers, scanners etc. There are three types of network cables; coaxial, twisted-pair, and fiber-optic (refer to Figure 4.1).

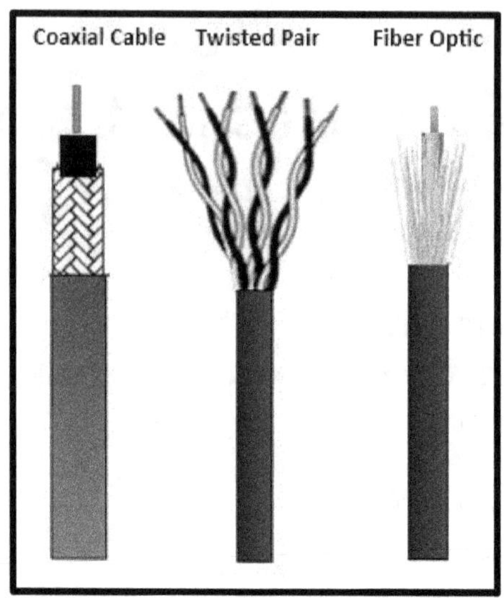

Figure 4.1 Types of Networking Cables

2. **Registered Jack 45 or RJ45**. A common data networking interface attached at the end of twisted wire pairs and an 8-pin modular jack. RJ-45 is used for Ethernet and Token Ring networks to connect UTP cable to network devices such as NIC, hub, switch, or router (refer to Figure 4.2).

Figure 4.2 RJ45 Connectors

3. **Modular Jack**. Also known as Keystone Jack Module or I/O Jack. A standardized snap-in package for mounting connectors into a keystone wall plate or a patch panel (refer to Figure 4.3).

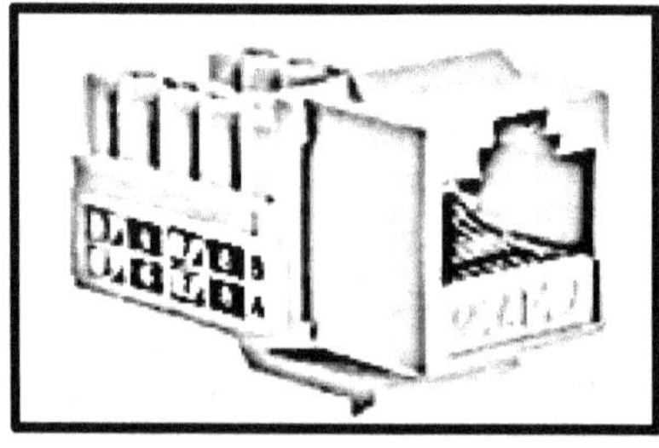

Figure 4.3 Modular Jack

4. **Modular Box**. Also known as *Keystone Wall Plate*. It is a surface mounted box used in a commercial and industrial building to cleanly attach network cables (refer to Figure 4.4). It is commonly used in a structured network in a building.

Figure 4.4 Modular Box

5. **Patch Panel**. Patch panel is made of multiple network ports to connect incoming and outgoing lines — including those for local area networks (refer to Figure 4.5). It can provide a simple, neat, and easy-to-manage cabling solution.

Figure 4.5 Patch Panel

6. **Cable Raceway**. Also known *as PVC molding, cable cover and cable concealer.* It hides cables and protect them from pets and children. It also make cables tight, make your homes or office look neat and clean (see Figure 4.6).

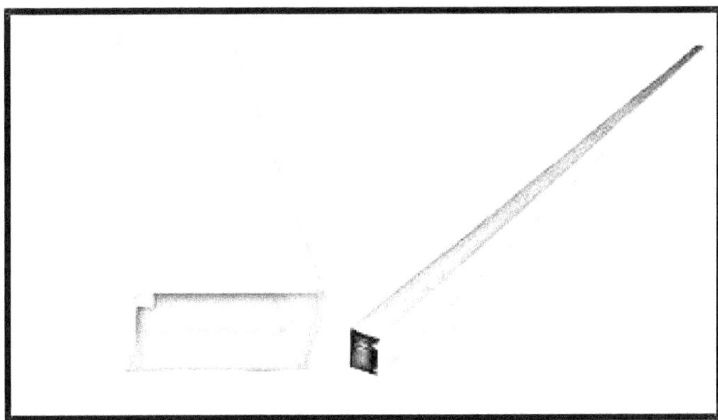

Figure 4.6 Cable Raceway

7. **Network Rack or cabinet**. A metal frame chassis that holds and secures various computer network devices like servers, routers, switches, access points, and modems (see Figure 4.7).

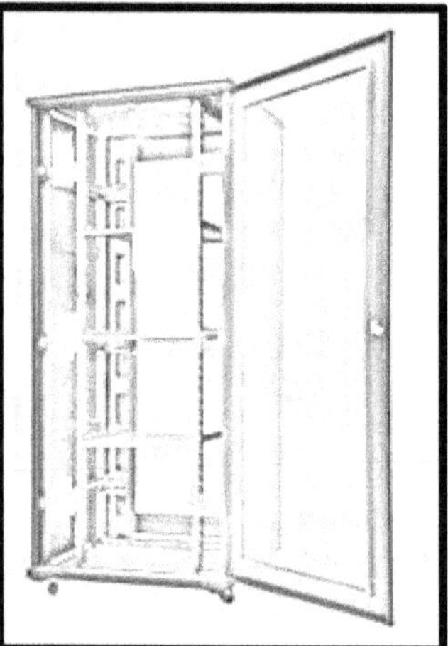

Figure 4.7 Network Rack

8. **Cable Ties**. A *cable tie* is a type of fastener used for holding items together, most commonly electrical cables or wires (see Figure 4.8).

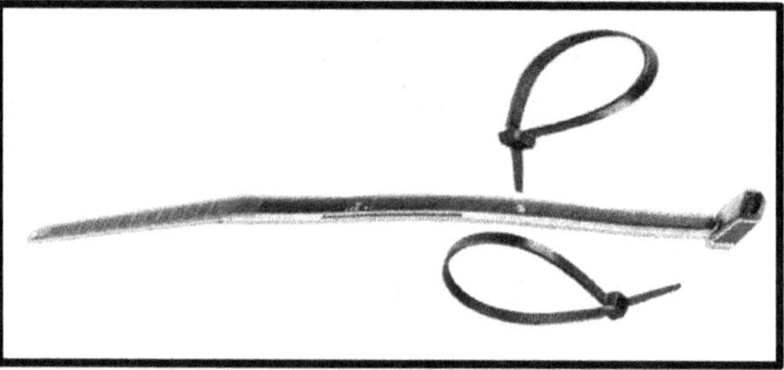

Figure 4.8 Cable Ties

NETWORK TOOLS

Creating and maintaining a wired network requires the use of many tools to maintain and troubleshoot it. The following basic tools are needed by computer technicians in performing this task.

1. **Crimping Tool** - This tool is used to attach the RJ45 connector to the end of the cable. Typically, this tool also includes a wire-cutter and wire-stripper (refer to Figure 4.9).

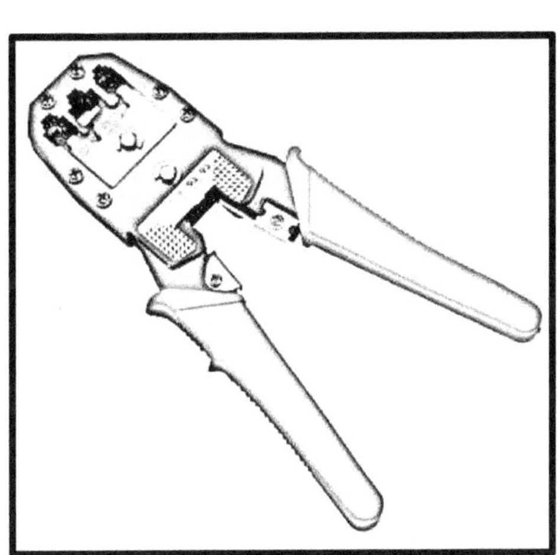

Figure 4.9 Crimping Tool

2. **Wire Cutter**. This tool is used to cut the network cable of the required length. A twisted-pair wire cutter usually includes additional blades for stripping the wire (refer to Figure 4.10).

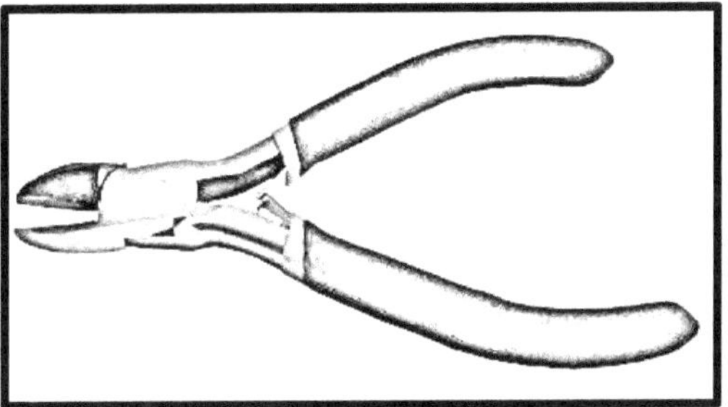

Figure 4.10 Wire Cutter

3. **Wire Stripper**. This tool is used to remove the insulation or protective coating of the network cable (refer to Figure 4.11) . *Typically, all standard twisted-pair wire cutters are equipped with wire-strippers.*

Figure 4.11 Wire Stripper

4. **Punch Down Tool**. A punch down tool, also called a krone tool, is used to connect network cable to a patch panel, keystone jack module, or I/O jack (refer to Figure 12).

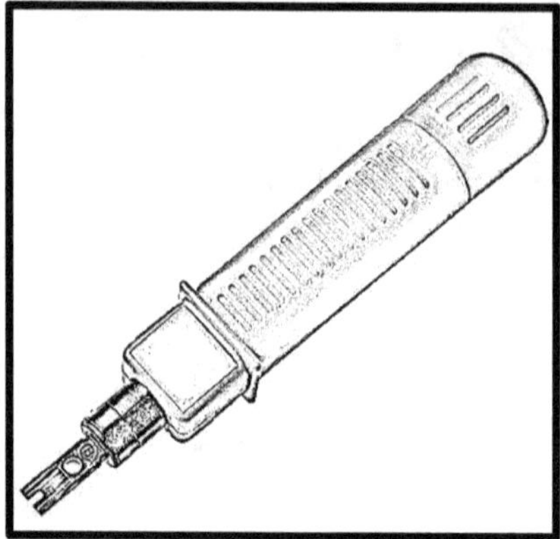

Figure 4.12 Punch Down Tool

5. **LAN Tester**. Also known as network cable tester. This electronic tool is used to verify the existence of a continuity of signal between the ends of the cable. It also verifies the correct wiring of connectors on the cable (refer to Figure 4.13).

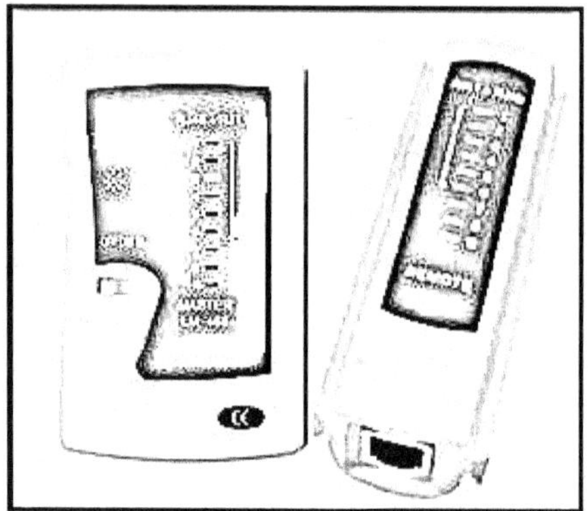

Figure 4.13 LAN Tester

6. **Loopback Plug.** A loopback cable is also known as a loopback plug or loopback adapter, which is a plug used to test physical ports to identify network issues. It provides a simple but effective way of testing the transmission capability and receiver sensitivity of network equipment (refer to Figure 4.12)

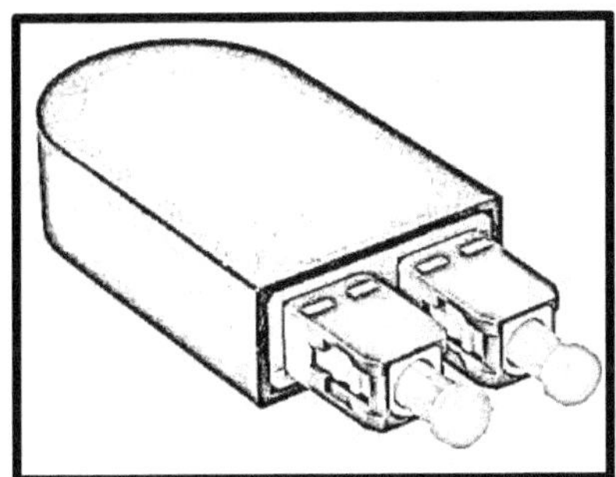
Figure 4.12 Loopback Plug

NETWORK DEVICES

In a computer network, network devices play an important role in transmitting and receiving data. Each networking device has various functions. They often perform a variety of tasks in different segments of the computer network.

1. **Hub.** A network hub is a device that broadcasts data to every computer connected to it (refer to Figure 4.13). Because it cannot tell where the information came from or where it is going, it sends the data to all the computers linked to it, including the one that sent it. A hub can either send or receive data, but not at the same time.

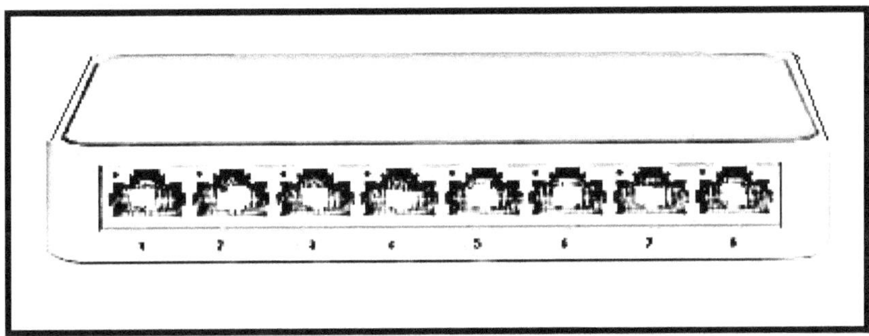
Figure 4.13 Hub

2. **Switch.** The switch functions similarly to hub, but it remembers the origin and intended destination of the data they collect, allowing them to send it only to the computers that are expected to receive it (refer to Figure 4.14). The switch can send and receive data at the same time, allowing it to send data more quickly than hub. It is commonly called an "intelligent hub".

Figure 4.14 Switch

3. Modem. Short for "Modulator-Demodulator." It converts analog signal to digital signal and vice versa. It receives information from your ISP through the phone lines, optical fiber, or coaxial cable in your home or office and converts it into a digital signal that a computer can recognize. Figure 4.15 shows the typical modem used by an ISP company to provide internet access to homes and offices.

Figure 4.15 Modem

4. Router. It is a device that enables computers to communicate and transfer data between two networks, such as your home network and the Internet (refer to Figure 4.16). Routers can analyze the data sent over a network, change how it is packaged, and send it to another network or over a different network.

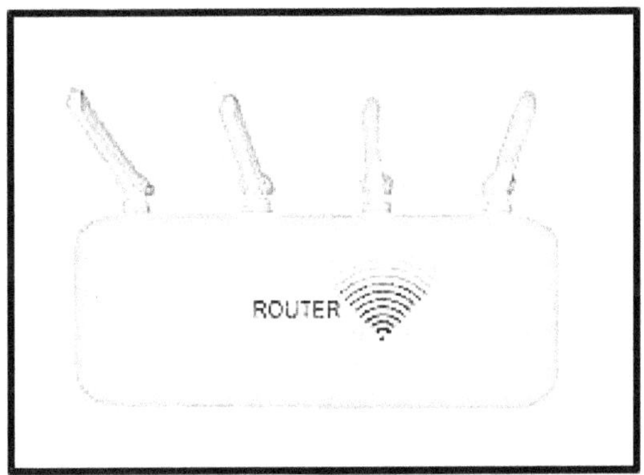

Figure 4.16 Router

5. **Wireless Access Point (WAP) Or Access Point (AP).** An access point (also called basepoint) is a device that creates a wireless local area network, or WLAN in your home or office (refer to Figure 4.17). An access point connects to a wired router, switch, or hub through an Ethernet cable, and projects a Wi-Fi signal to a specified location.

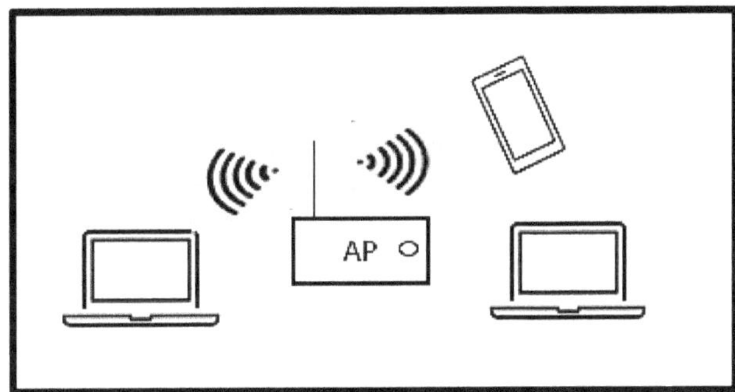

Figure 4.17 Wireless Access Point

6. **WIFI Repeater / Extender.** Both Wi-Fi repeaters and Wi-Fi extenders increase your Wi-Fi signal and range, but in different ways. A Wi-Fi extender links to your router directly and establishes a new Wi-Fi network. A Wi-Fi repeater links wirelessly to your network and rebroadcasts your current network signal (refer to Figure 4.18).

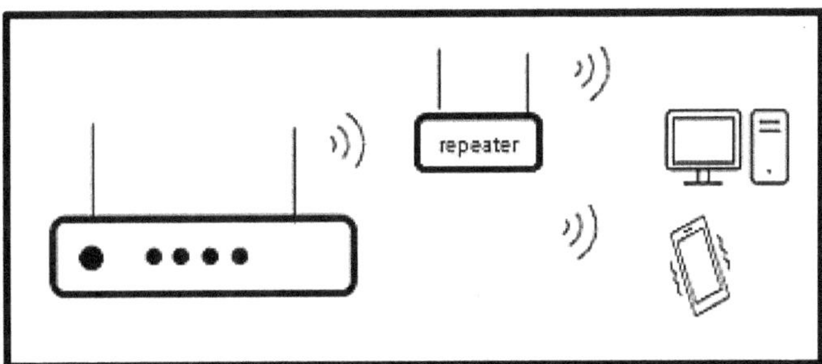

Figure 4.18 WIFI Repeater

7. **Bridge.** A network bridge connects two separate local area networks as shown in Figure 4.19. The network bridge enables communication between the two networks and provides a way for them to work as a single network that uses the same protocol.

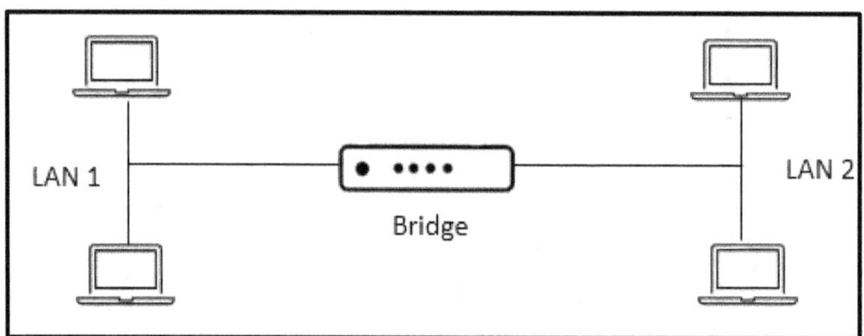

Figure 4.19 Network Bridge

8. **Network Interface Card (NIC).** As shown in Figure 4.20, the Network Interface card is a circuit board installed in a computer that provides a dedicated network connection to the computer. It is also called network interface controller, network adapter or LAN Card. NIC allows both wired and wireless communications. Without NIC, a computer cannot connect over a network.

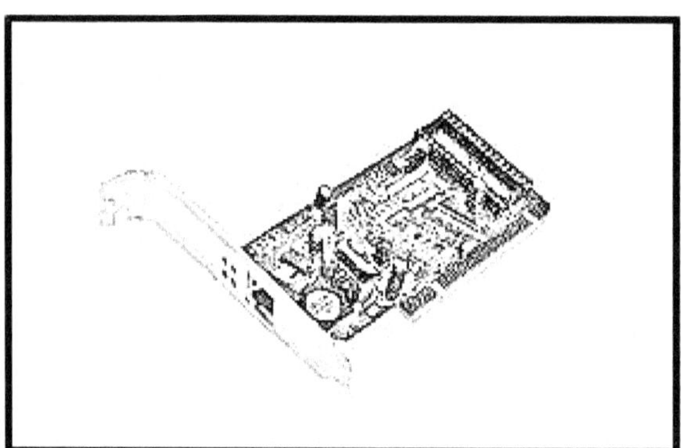

Figure 4.20 Network Interface Card (NIC)

Chapter 5

TRANSMISSION MEDIA

In this chapter, you will be familiarizing yourself with different types of transmission media, their characteristics, and their advantages and disadvantages. Once you have understood this topic, it will be easier for you to decide on the type and scope of cabling you need to consider in building your computer network for your organization. After going through this chapter, you are expected to:

1. identify the various type of different transmission media;
2. enumerate and demonstrate understanding of different types of guided and unguided media;
3. evaluate the advantages and disadvantages of different types of guided and unguided media; and
4. appreciate the importance of transmission media in building computer networks.

In building computer networks, there are many different types of transmission media to choose from. Depending on the networking situation and specifications, different cable types can be needed. When determining which form of transmission media to use in constructing a computer network, there are many factors to consider.

Transmission Media

Network Transmission media, or network media is a communication pathway that transmits the information from the sender to the receiver.

Types of Transmission Media

Transmission media is classified into two types namely *Guided* (wired) media and *Unguided* (wireless) media. The medium characteristics of wired media are more significant but, in wireless media the signal characteristics are more important.

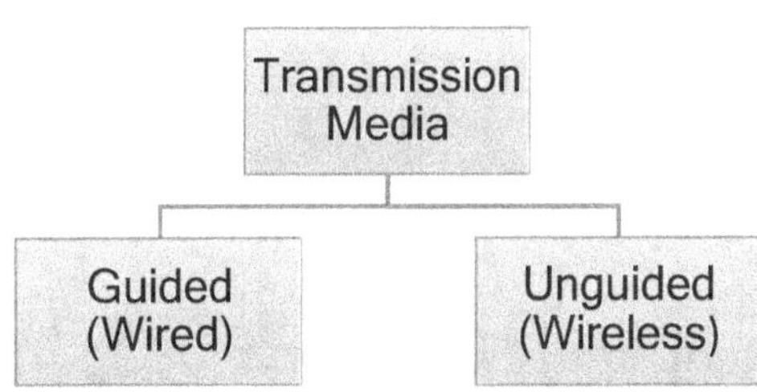

Figure 5.1 Types of Transmission Media

Guided Media

This type of transmission media is also known as wired or bounded media. It provides the physical medium through which signals are transmitted from one device to another. The main features of guided media include secure, high-speed, and used in small distances.

Unguided (wireless) Media

This type of media does not use a physical medium to send data from one device to another. Because of this, it is frequently referred to as wireless media. Unlike guided media, it uses air as a transmission medium rather than wire or cable. Wireless signals travel across the air and are picked up and interpreted by antennas.

Classification of Guided Media
1. Twisted Pair Cable
2. Coaxial Cable
3. Fiber Optic Cable

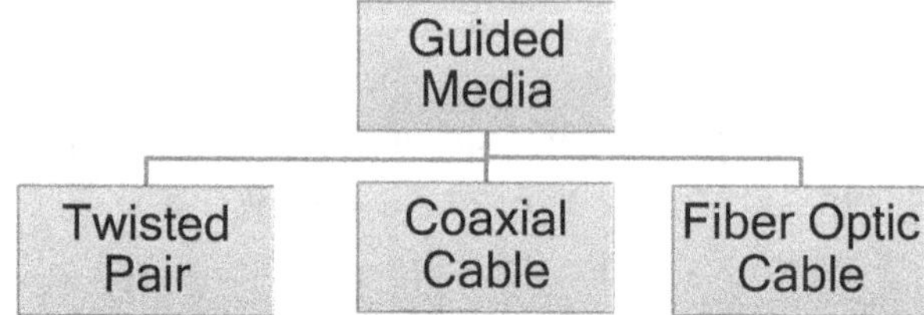

Figure 5.2 Classification of Transmission Media

Twisted Pair Cable

This type of cable is created by twisting two separate insulated wires together and running them parallel to each other in a twisted pattern. This cable is the most common and is less expensive than others. It is small, inexpensive, and simple to install, and it supports a wide range of network types. It is commonly used for telecommunications and most modern Ethernet networks.

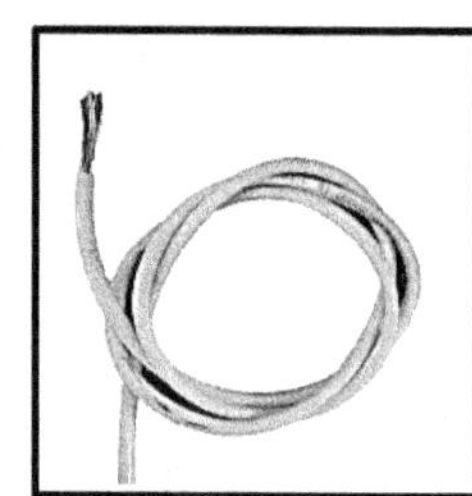

Figure 5.3 Twisted Pair Cable

Why are the paired wires twisted?

Wires are twisted to minimize the noise, interruption, and crosstalk that occur in any transmission. When the wires are twisted, some noise signals travel in the same direction as data signals, while others travel in opposite directions. As a result of the various twists, the external waves cancel out.

Types of Twisted Pair Cable

Shown in Figure 5.4, twisted-pair cables has two types are:

1. **Unshielded Twisted Pair (UTP).** This cable is widely used in computer networks and telecommunications industries as Ethernet cables and telephone wires.
2. **Shielded Twisted Pair (STP).** This twisted-pair cabling has additional shielding to reduce crosstalk and other forms of electromagnetic interference (EMI).

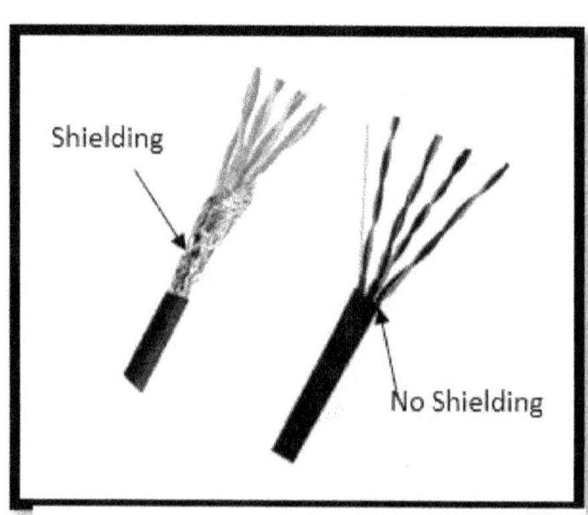

Figure 5.4 Types of Twisted Pair

Coaxial Cable

This cable has an external plastic cover and two parallel conductors (inner and outer), each with its own safety cover. The inner conductor (center) is the primary signal carrier. The outer conductor makes the coaxial cable less susceptible to noise. This cable is used to relay data in two different modes: baseband and broadband. This cable is commonly used in cable television and analog television networks.

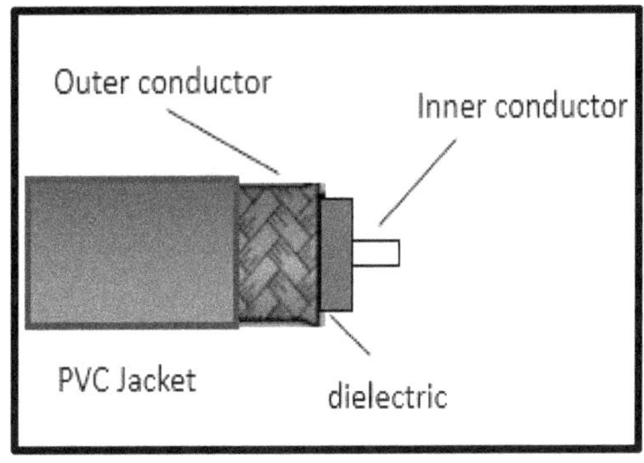

Figure 5.5 Coaxial Cable

The advantages of the coaxial cable include high bandwidth, good noise immunity, low cost, and simple installation. The downside of this cable is, if it fails, it may disrupt the whole network.

What is the main reason why coaxial cables are less vulnerable to noise than twisted pair cables?

Types of Coaxial Cable

1. **Baseband**. This is a 50 ohm (Ω) coaxial cable that is used for digital transmission. It is mostly used for LANs. It sends only one signal at a time at a very high speed. The main disadvantage is that it needs amplification every 1000 feet.

2. **Broadband**. This uses analog transmission on standard cable television cabling. It transmits several simultaneous signals using different frequencies. It is mostly used for WANs.

Fiber Optic Cable

This cable contains an insulated casing of glass fiber strands. It is made for long-distance, high-speed data networking, and telecommunications. It uses light pulses provided by small lasers or light-emitting diodes to carry communication signals. It has a higher bandwidth than wired cables and can relay data over longer distances.

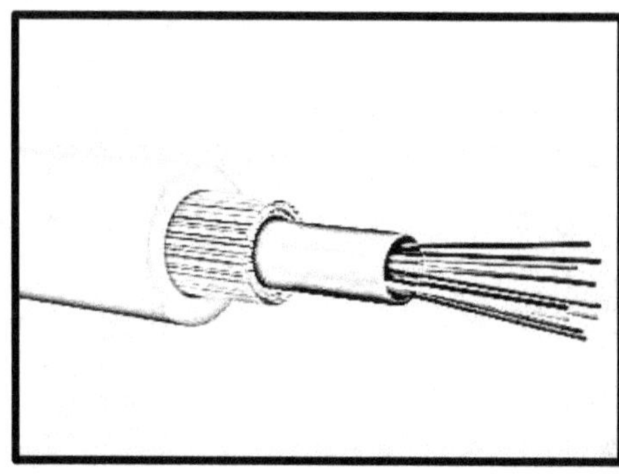

Figure 5.6 Fiber Optic

Types of Fiber Optic Cable
1. **Single mode**. This cable has a narrow diameter center that only one mode of light can propagate through it. As a result, the number of light reflections produced as light passes through the center reduces, reducing attenuation and allowing the signal to travel further. Telcos usually use this cable in long-distance, higher-bandwidth networks.
2. **Multimode.** This cable allows several modes of light to spread because it has a large diametral core. As a result, the number of light reflections generated as light passes through the center increases, allowing more data to pass through at a given time. It is typically used for short distance, data, and audio/video applications in local area networks (LANs).

Unguided Media

Unguided Media or wireless transmission media is preferred by many people because it is more convenient than installing cables. Furthermore, companies use wireless transmission media in areas where installing cables is impractical.

Classification of Unguided Media
1. Infrared
2. Broadcast Radio
3. Cellular Radio
4. Microwaves
5. Satellite

Infrared (IR). It is a wireless communication medium that uses infrared light waves to transmit signals. Infrared Data Association (rDA) ports are found on many *personal computers* and *tablets*, including *mice*, *printers*, and *smartphones*, and enable data to be transferred from one device to another using infrared light waves. To communicate, infrared devices must frequently be within 5 meters of each other (refer to Figure 5.7).

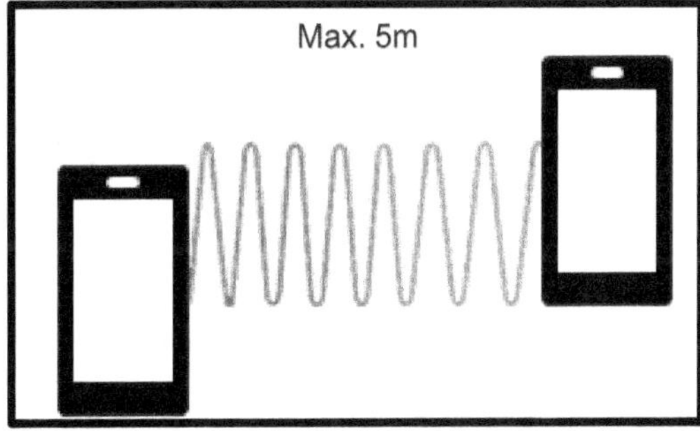

Figure 5.7 Infrared

Figure 5.8 Broadcast Radio

Broadcast Radio. It is a form of wireless transmission that sends radio signals over long distances, such as between cities, regions, and countries, as well as short distances, such as within an office or home (refer to Figure 5.8). Broadcast radio signals are used in *Bluetooth, Wi-Fi, WiMAX*, and UWB networking technologies.

Bluetooth. It uses short-range radio waves to transmit data between two devices (refer to Figure 5.9). The data transfer between devices is at a rate of 1Mbps. To communicate, devices must be within about 10 meters (33 feet). Bluetooth transmission speeds and range are usually slower than Wi-Fi (the wireless local area network that you may have in your home).

Figure 5.9 Bluetooth

WIFI (Wireless Infidelity). It uses short-range radio waves to provide wireless high-speed internet access (refer to Figure 5.9). The data transfer between devices is at a rate of 11-54 Mbps. To communicate, devices must be within about 30 meters (100 feet). It transmits data from your wireless network to Wi-Fi enabled devices such as your TV, smartphone, tablet, and computer using radio waves. Your devices and personal information may be vulnerable to hackers, cyber-attacks, and other hazards since they communicate through airwaves.

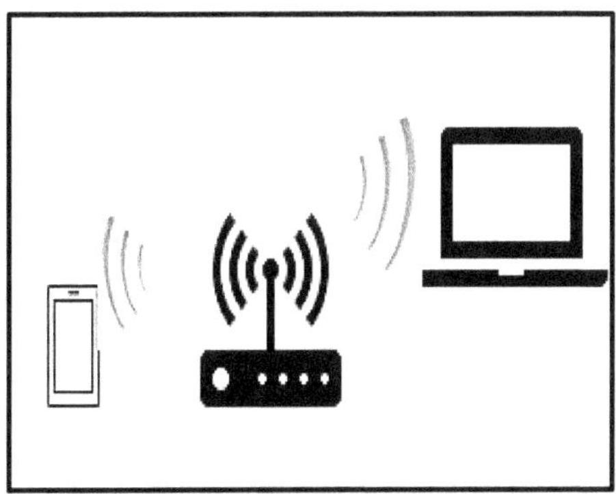

Figure 5.9 Bluetooth

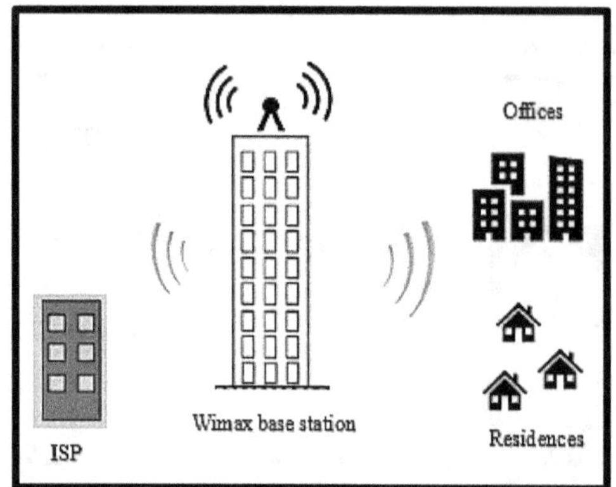

Figure 5.10 WiMAX

WiMAX (Worldwide Interoperability for Microwave Access). It is a telecommunications technology that allows users to send and receive wireless data over long distances in several ways, ranging from point-to-point connections to complete mobile cellular service (refer to Figure 5.10). It is a broadband connection to the Internet at service quality and an alternative to cable and DSL.

UWB (Ultra-Wideband). It is a short-range wireless communication technology like Wi-Fi or Bluetooth. Figure 5.11 shows that UWB transmits radio waves of short pulses over a spectrum of frequencies ranging from 3.1 to 10.5 GHz. It lets you pinpoint the exact location of phones, key fobs, wallets and tracking tags, helping you find lost dogs or automatically unlock your car.

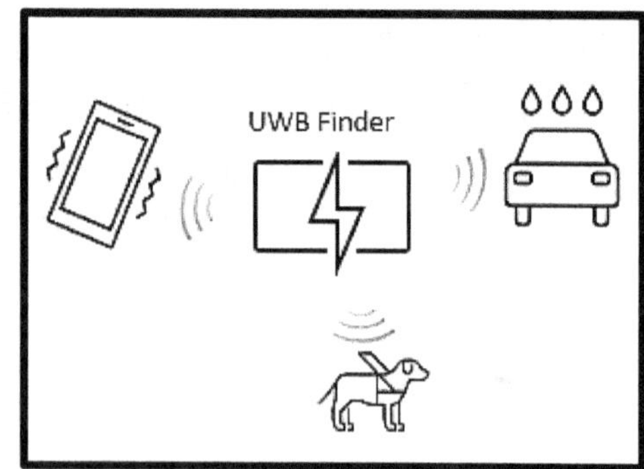

Figure 5.11 Ultra-Wideband

Figure 5.12 Cellular Radio

Cellular Radio. It is a form of broadcast radio that is commonly used in mobile communications, such as cellular modems and cell phones (see Figure 5.11). A mobile phone is a telephone that transmits voice and digital data messages using high-frequency radio waves.

Microwaves. These are radio waves that transmit information at a high rate. Microwave transmission, also known as fixed wireless, entails the transmission of signals from one microwave station to another. Figure 5.13 shows that each station consists of a reflective dish that houses the antenna, transceivers, and other microwave communications equipment. Microwaves are used to clear potential obstacles such as structures or mountains.

Figure 5.13 Microwaves

Satellite. A communications satellite is a space station that receives microwave signals

Figure 5.14 Satellite

from an earth-based station, amplifies (strengthens) the signals, and broadcasts the signals to any number of earth-based microwave stations over a large region (refer to Figure 5.14). Other devices that can function as earth-based stations include smartphones and GPS receivers. Satellites can be used for transmission of program video, voice, or data signals almost anywhere on earth, no matter how remote the location. They provide multi-channel capabilities, wide bandwidths, and high data rates.

CHAPTER 6

ETHERNET CABLE CONFIGURATIONS

After completing this chapter, you will understand Ethernet cable configurations. Understanding the Ethernet cable configurations allows you to start setting-up and configuring your local area network. After going through this module, you are expected to:

1. identify the various type of Ethernet network cables for Local Area Network;
2. demonstrate understanding of different types of cable configurations;
3. appreciate the importance of following the steps for creating network cable; in accordance with established procedures and system requirements; and
4. perform cable splicing for network cable installation.

Cabling is the backbone of every computer network. Computers, routers, hubs, switches, and storage systems all require network cables to link and transmit data and other information. It can be compared to the veins in the human body. They are data transporters that allow information to flow from one device to another.

Ethernet cables are the backbone of any computer network. It helps you to provide faster speed, more consistent and more reliable transfer of data than WIFI.

Local Area Network (LAN)

A local area network (LAN) is a computer network that links computers in a specific geographic area, such as a home, school, laboratory, university campus, or office building.

Types of LAN Technology

1. **Ethernet**. It is the standard way to connect computers on a local area network over a wired connection. Its architecture is based on the premise that many computers can access it and submit data at any time. Ethernet is popular because it provides a good balance of speed, cost, and ease of installation.

2. **Fast Ethernet.** It offers faster video, multimedia, graphics, and Internet browsing throughput, as well as improved error detection and correction.

3. **Gigabit Ethernet**. It is considered a must for some professionals and hobbyists who need the highest possible data streaming speed on the market. Mainly, video creators, 4K video streamers, and video game streamers use this type of network technology.

4. **10 Gigabit Ethernet**. This is the fastest and most recent Ethernet standards. The 10 Gigabit Ethernet, unlike other Ethernet networks, is completely dependent on optical fiber connections.

Ethernet Cable

An Ethernet cable is a set of eight copper wires wrapped together in a single outer insulated cover (refer to Figure 6.1). It is the common type of network cable used in guided (wired) networks. It connects devices such as PCs, routers, and switches within a local area network.

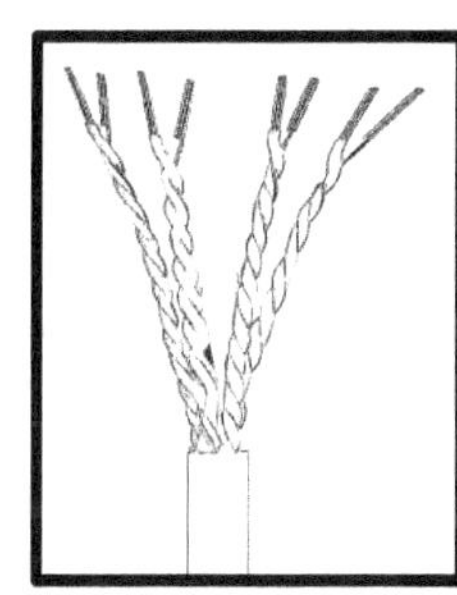

Figure 6.1 Ethernet Cable

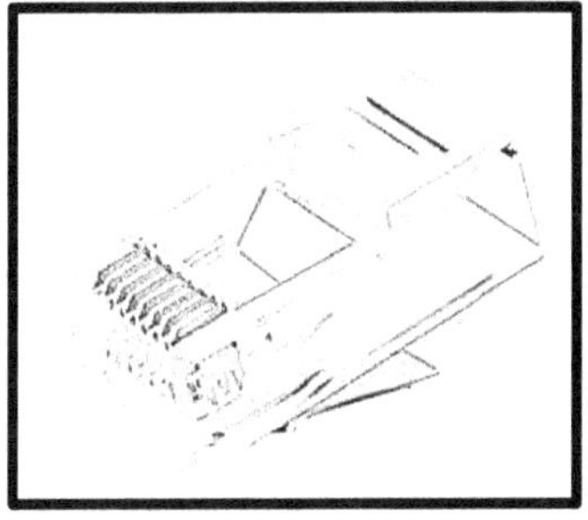

Figure 6.2 Ethernet Cable

RJ45 JACK

A modular connector that makes it easy to install or remove a cable from any Ethernet device. It is commonly referred to as RJ45. It is made of clear or translucent plastic used for terminating twisted pair cable, a process known as *wire termination* (refer to Figure 6.2).

Ethernet Port

An Ethernet port (also called LAN port, Ethernet jack, LAN socket, and network port) is an opening on network devices that Ethernet cables plug into (refer to Figure 6.3). Its purpose is to connect devices to a computer network.

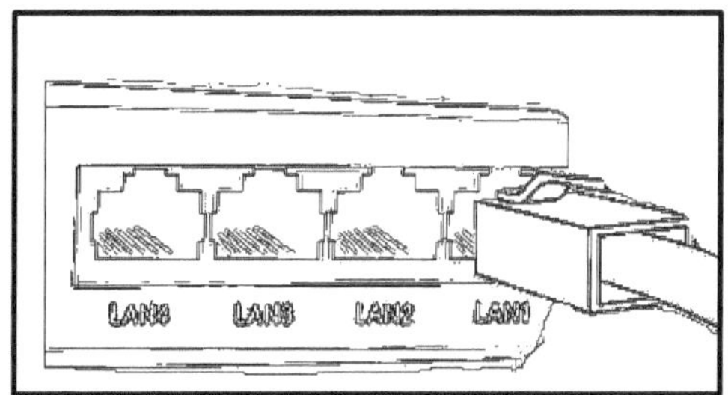

Figure 6.3 Ethernet Port

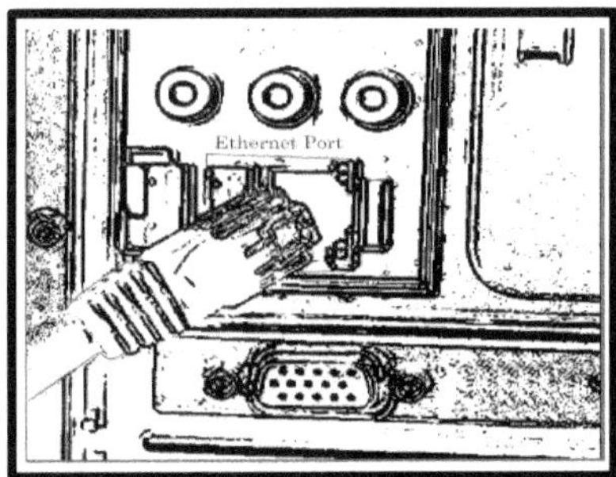

Figure 6.4 Computer Ethernet Port

Ethernet Ports on Computers

Most desktop and laptop computers include one built-in Ethernet port that is used to connect these devices to a wired network (refer to Figure 6.4). A computer's built-in Ethernet port is connected to its internal Ethernet network adapter, called an **Ethernet card** (also called network adaptor, and network interface card), which is attached to the motherboard.

Types of Ethernet Cabling

Coaxial, twisted pair, and fiber-optic cabling are the three most common forms of Ethernet cabling. But twisted pair cabling is the most common form of cabling in today's local area networks.

Twisted Pair Ethernet Cable

Two separate insulated copper wires are twisted together and run in parallel to form a twisted pair cable (refer to Figure 6.5). One wire transmits data, while the other serves as a ground reference. Copper wires normally have a diameter of 1mm.

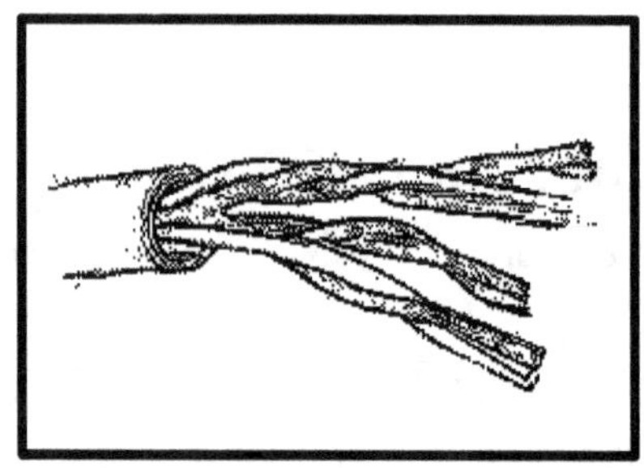

Figure 6.5 Twisted Pair Ethernet Cable

Ethernet Cabling Category

There are a variety of Ethernet cable options available, each with its own function and application. If you want to learn everything there is to know about Ethernet cables, you must first understand the cable category and its use. You should go for the higher-quality cable because it will be thicker, quicker, and better suited to your needs.

Category 1. CAT1 is typically used for telephone wires. This type of wire is not capable of supporting computer network traffic and is not twisted (refer to Figure 6.6).

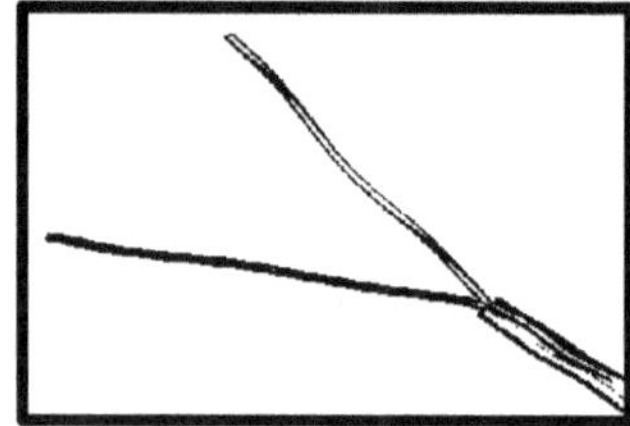

Figure 6.6 CAT 1 Cable

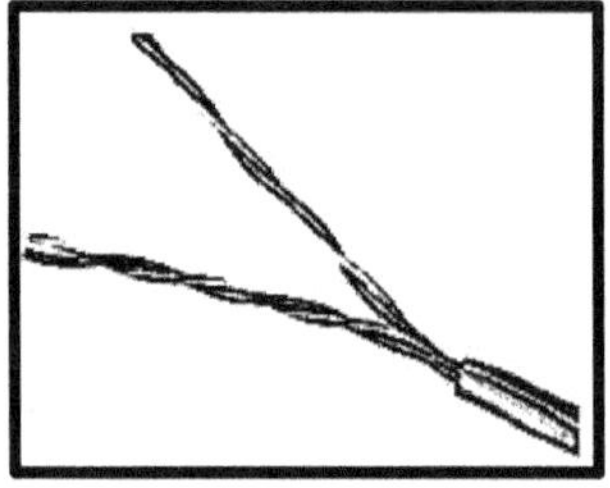

Figure 6.7 CAT 2 Cable

Category 2. CAT2 is unshielded twisted pair cabling used mostly for token ring networks, supporting speeds up to 4 Mbps only (refer to Figure 6.7). It is a grade of unshielded twisted pair cabling used for telephone and data communications.

Category 3. CAT3 cable is an earlier generation of cable consisting of 2, 3, or 4 copper pairs. It is still used for 2-line telephone systems and 10BASE-T computer networks. It's also used for alarm system installation and other related tasks. It is known as station wire. It has data transmission up to 16 MHz or 10 Mbps

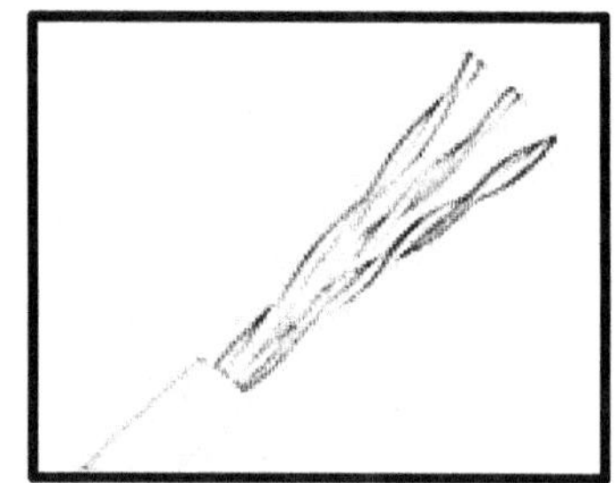

Figure 6.8 CAT 3 Cable

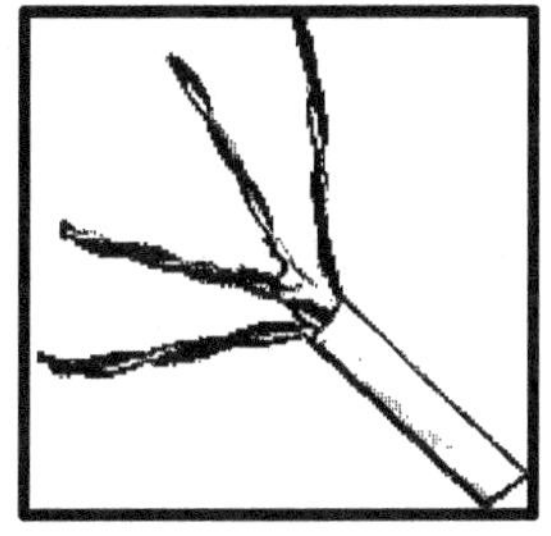

Category 4. Eight copper wires are twisted together in four unshielded twisted pairs to make CAT4 cable (refer to Figure 6.9). It's used in voice and data-transferring telephone networks with data transmission up to 20 MHz or 16 Mbps.

Figure 6.9 CAT 4 Cable

Category 5. CAT5 cable consists of four twisted pairs of copper wire terminated by an RJ-45 connector (refer to Figure 6.10). This cable is used in both home and business networks and can transmit data at speeds of up to 100 Mbps. The maximum recommended length of a CAT5 cable is 100 meters.

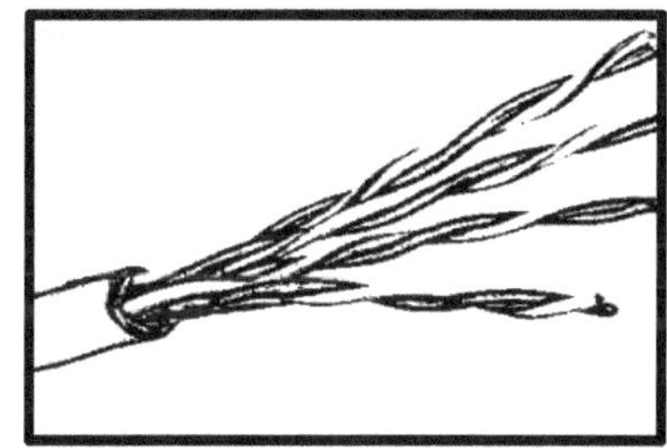

Figure 6.10 CAT 5 Cable

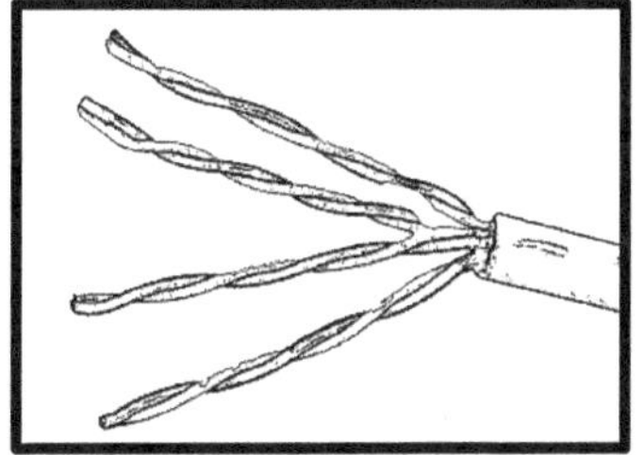

Figure 6.11 CAT 5e Cable

Category 5e. CAT5e is a twisted pair cable and one of the most popular cablings used for deployments because of its ability to support Gigabit speeds at a cost-effective price (refer to Figure 6.11).

Category 6. CAT6 cabling is a twisted cable that can transmit data at speeds of up to 10 Gbps and at frequencies of up to 250MHz. These cables have two or three twists per centimeter and are more strongly twisted (refer to Figure 6.12). When transmitting at 10 Gbps speeds, it only supports 37-55 meters.

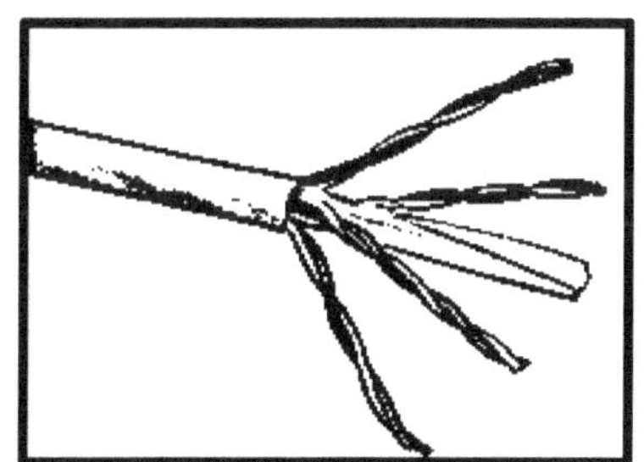

Figure 6.12 CAT 6 Cable

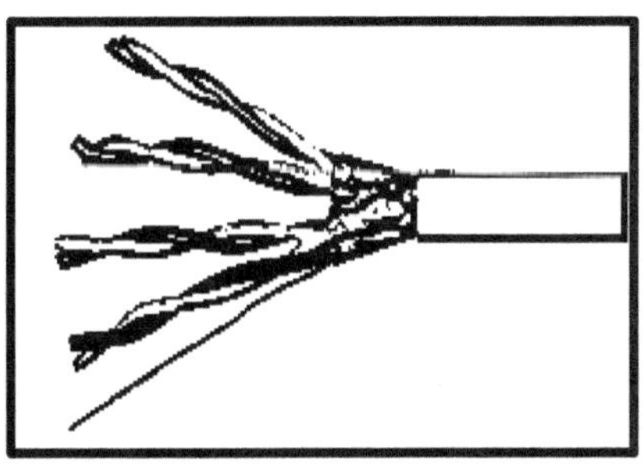

Figure 6.13 CAT 6a Cable

Category 6a. CAT6a ethernet cable consists of 4 unshielded twisted pairs and no outer shielding (refer to Figure 6.13). It supports bandwidth frequencies of up to 500 MHz CAT6a cabling is thicker compared to CAT6, making it less flexible. As a result, it is better suited to industrial environments at a lower cost.

Category 7. CAT7 can transmit up to 40 Gbps at 50 meters and even 100 Gbps at 15 meters. This type of Ethernet cable has a lot of shielding, which reduces signal attenuation (refer to Figure 6.14). It is suited for use in Datacenters and large Enterprise networks. CAT7, on the other hand, has not been accepted as a telecommunications cable standard.

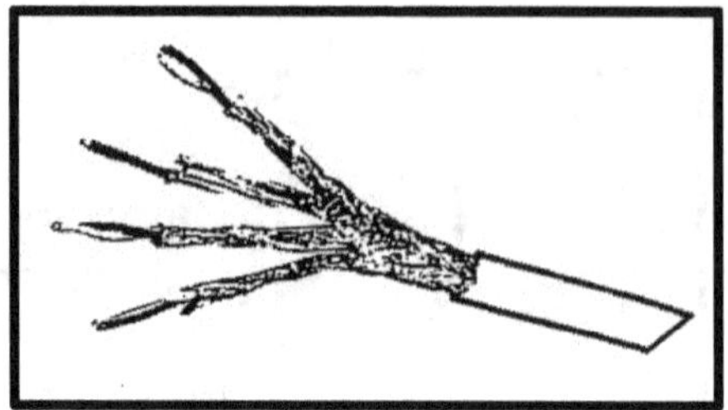

Figure 6.14 CAT 7 Cable

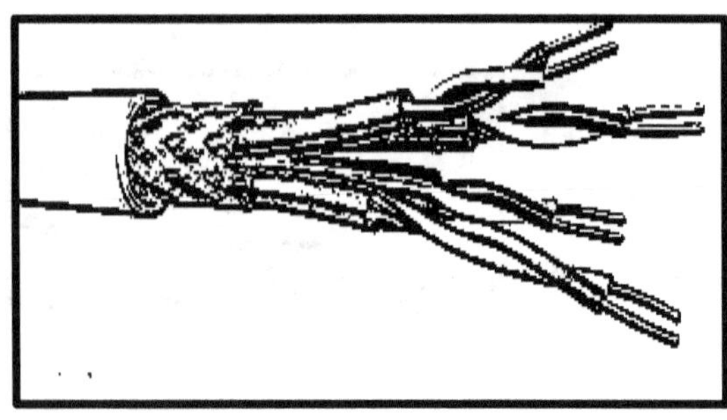

Figure 6.15 CAT 7 Cable

Category 8: CAT8 cable is capable of transmitting data at up to 2000MHz. It supports 25/40GBASE-T Gigabit Ethernet and is designed for high-bandwidth data center applications. This form of cable is ideal for short distances between units. Backward compatibility exists between CAT8 cables and previous Ethernet cable groups (refer to Figure 6.15).

Ethernet Wiring Standard

RJ45 connector is a modular connector used for terminating twisted pair cable. There are two ways to arrange the wiring inside an Ethernet cable when it comes to the actual wiring. This arrangement dictates how the connector is terminated – a process called *pinout*.

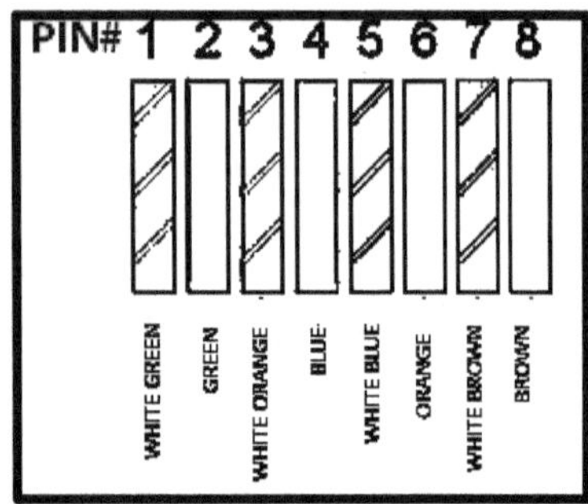

Figure 6.16 T568A Color Sequence

1. T568A. Since it is backward compatible with both one pair and two pair wiring schemes, this wiring pattern is known as the preferred wiring scheme. The order of color combinations is white/green, green, white/orange, blue, white/blue, orange, white/brown, and brown (refer to Figure 6.16)

2. T568B. This wiring pattern is considered the most widely used wiring scheme. The order of color combinations is white/orange, orange, white/green, blue, blue/white, green, white/brown, and brown (refer to Figure 6.17

NOTE: Odd-numbered pins are always striped, even-numbered pins are always solid colored.

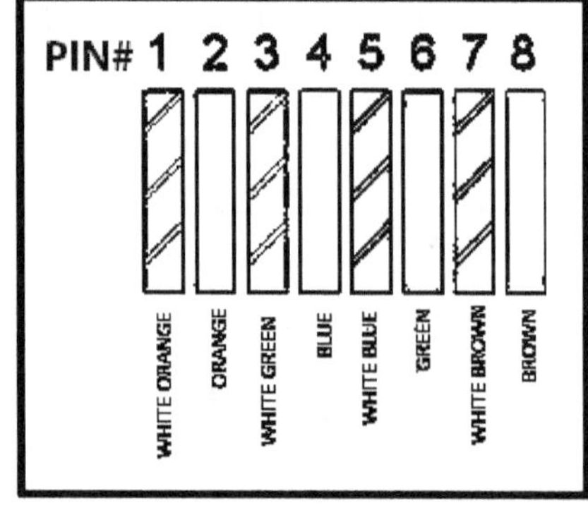

Figure 6.16 T568A Color Sequence

Types of Ethernet Cable Configuration

1. **Straight-through cable**. This twisted pair cable is also called a *patch cable*. It used RJ45 connectors at each end, and each had the same pinout. It is used in local area networks to connect two different network devices such as:
   a. Connecting a router to a hub
   b. Connecting a computer to a switch
   c. Connecting a LAN Port to a switch or computer
   d. Connecting other dissimilar networking devices

2. **Crossover cable.** This twisted pair cable uses RJ45 connectors at each end, where one end is a T568A pinout, and the other end is a T568B pinout. It is used to connect two similar network devices directly such as:
   a. Connecting a computer to a computer
   b. Connecting a router to a router
   c. Connecting a switch to a switch
   d. Connecting a hub to a hub
   e. Connecting a router to a PC because both devices have the same components.

How to create Ethernet Cable

To create ethernet cable you will need the following *tools* and *materials*:

1. **Crimping Tool**. This tool is used to attach the RJ45 Connector to the end of the network cable.

2. **Wire Stripper**. A tool used to strip the electrical insulation from wires.

3. **RJ45**. The modular connector used for terminating twisted pair cable.

4. **LAN Tester.** A device that tests the continuity of signal between two ends of a cable. It also checks for the correct wiring pattern.

Follow the following steps to create your ethernet cable:

Step 1: Remove the cable jacket about 1 inch down from the end. You can use wire strippers to do the work.

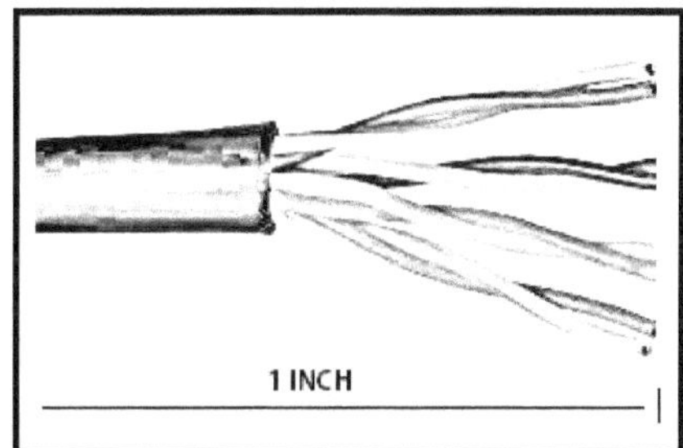

Step 2: Untwist and spread the wire apart.

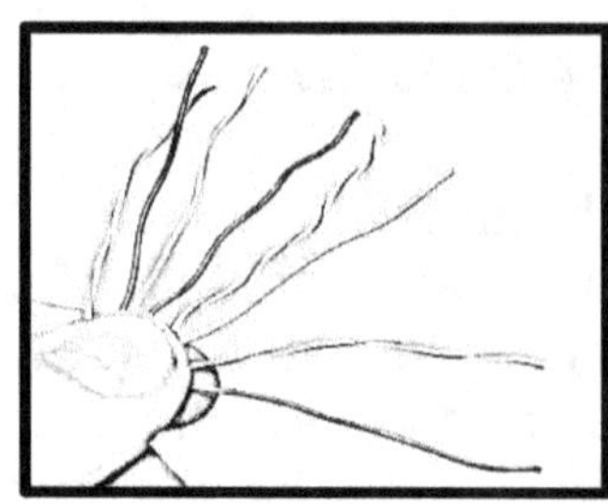

Step 3. Arrange the wires in the order (T568A or T568B) in which you want to crimp them.

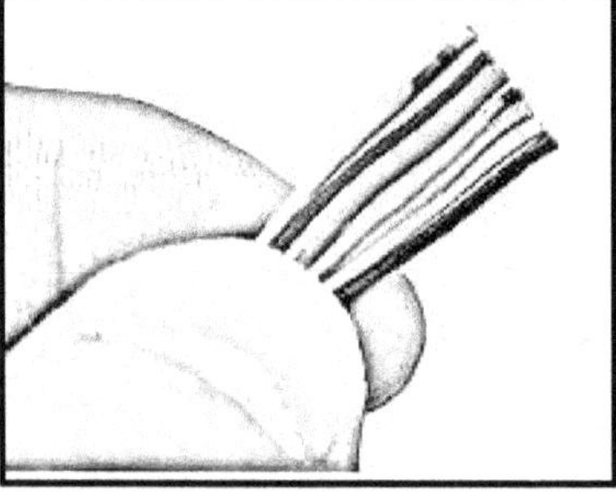

Step 4. From the cut sleeve to the end of the wires, make a straight cut through the 8 wires to shorten them to 1/2 inch (1.3 cm). The job will be done by a razor blade on the crimping tool.

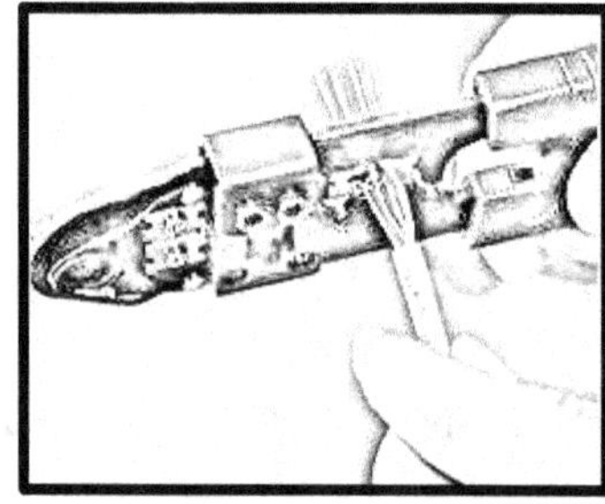

Step 5. Carefully push the wires into the RJ45 connector with care, making sure they are in a straight line. The wires should be able to hit the very edge.

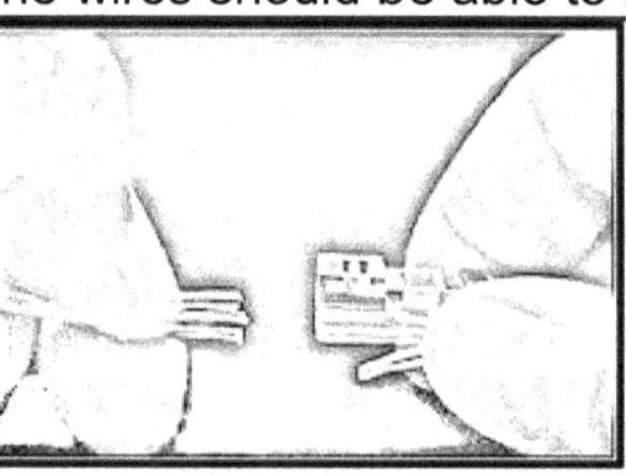

Step 6. Carefully insert the RJ45 connector into the Crimping Tool. Clinch down on the handle tightly.

Step 7: Repeat steps 1 to 6 on the other end of the cable.

Testing the Ethernet Cable
To test the ethernet cable we need to use a LAN tester or cable tester. You must plug both ends of the Ethernet cable into a LAN tester and see if it successfully transmits a signal. This device provides a level of assurance that the installed network cable provides the desired transmission capability to support the data communication within the local area network.

Steps in Testing an Ethernet Cable

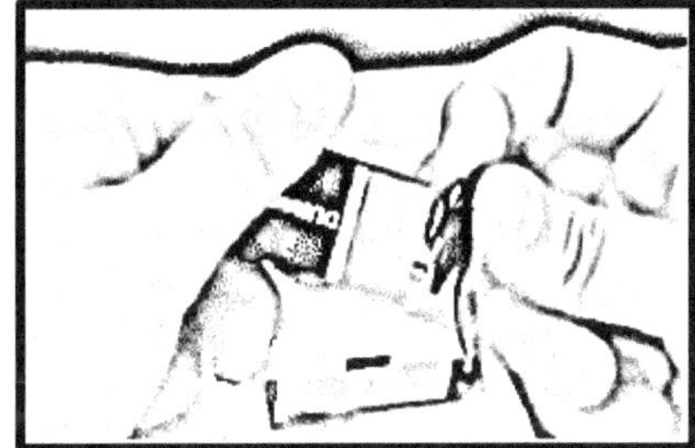

Step 1: Check your LAN Tester and make sure the battery is in the best shape. Most LAN Testers use 9V batteries. LAN Testers usually comes in 2 pieces, the main testing unit (TX) and a receiver unit (RX).

Step 2: Plug one end of the Ethernet cable into the RJ45 interface of RX until it clicks. This indicates that the cable is fully connected. It doesn't matter which end of the cable you insert into each port. Both ends are identical.

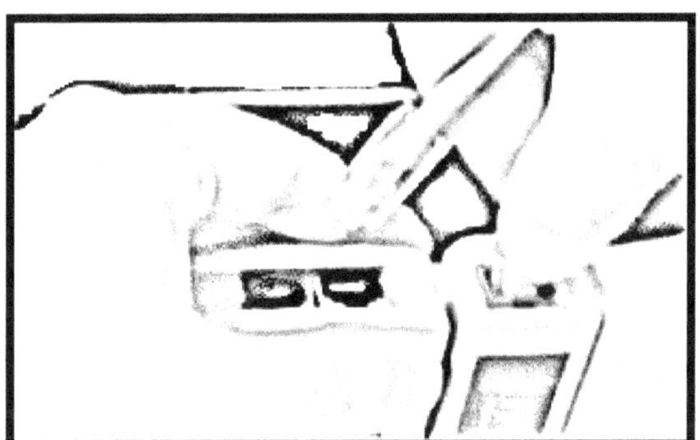

Step 3: Plug the other end into the RJ45 interface of the TX. Again, push the end of the cable until it clicks.

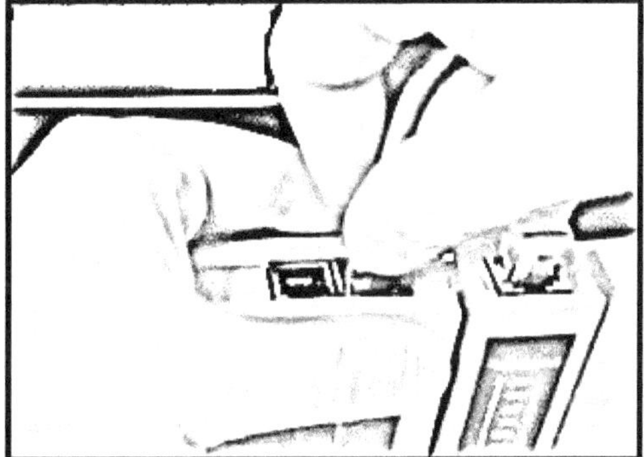

Step 4: Turn the tester on to begin the test. The tester will cycle through 8 positions, each represented by a light on the tester.

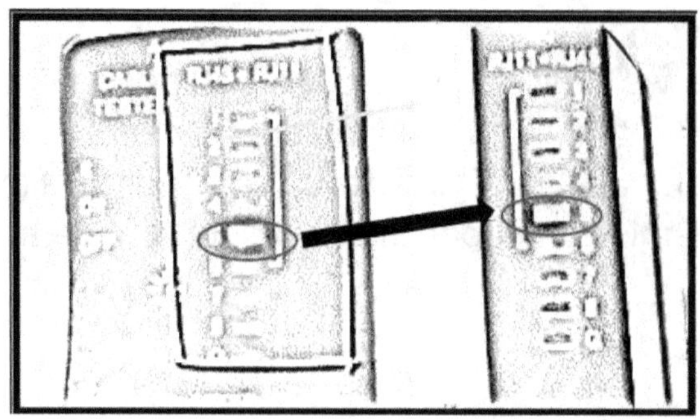

Straight-through Cable:

If all 8 positions light up on both TX and RX simultaneously, the cable is good. A short in the cable is indicated if any of the lights on either end do not light up.

Crossover Cable:
If you are testing a crossover cable, you must see the light runs on the following sequence:

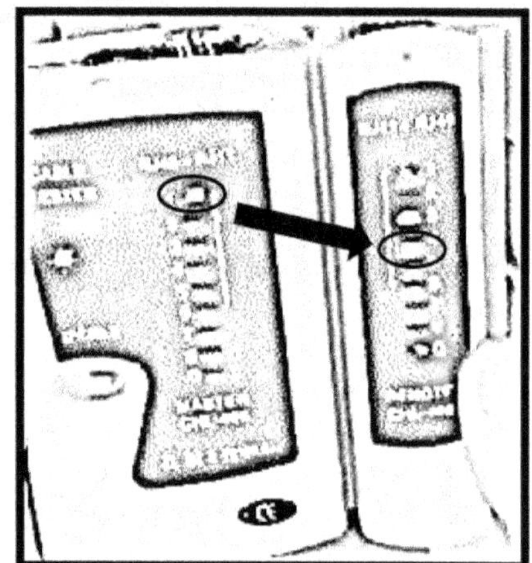

TX	RX
1	3
2	6
3	1
5	5
6	2
7	7
8	8

CHAPTER 7

CABLE MANAGEMENT

After completing this chapter, you will understand how to manage your network cabling system using patch panel and modular jack to create a visually pleasing and clean environment. After going through this module, you are expected to:

1. define and understand the concepts of cable management and structured cabling;
2. identify the various components of structured cabling;
3. demonstrate understanding of patch panel and modular jack;
4. appreciate the importance cable management in building computer network; and
5. perform cabling of patch panel and modular jack.

A well-managed network infrastructure not only leads to a high level of system performance, but it also has a lot of visual appeal. More significantly, effective network cable management will reduce operation costs and time while increasing network operation and maintenance versatility and flexibility. The major advantages, combined with the increased network agility and ability, and cabling density, make a comprehensive cable management solution.

Cable Management

It refers to the organization of Ethernet cables connected to network devices. Cables can quickly get tangled, making them difficult to deal with and, in some cases, causing devices to become unplugged inadvertently when attempting to pass a cable. This cabling situation is usually referred to as "cable spaghetti".

One end of a cable is usually terminated in a rack or cabinet. The other end of a cable ends at the computer of the end users at either end, the cable management requirements are different.

Structured cabling

It is a kind of network cabling solution that organizes the cable's setup. It also refers to the design and installation of a cabling system that will support multiple hardware uses to make it easier to manage as your network grows.

COMPONENTS OF STRUCTURED CABLING

1. **Entrance Facility**. It marks where the ISP's wiring ends and where your organization's wiring begins. In entrance facility, you'll find cabling, demarcation points or sometimes shortened to the "demarc.", connecting hardware and any other equipment to connect the outside provider's cabling to the private cabling (refer to Figure 7.1).

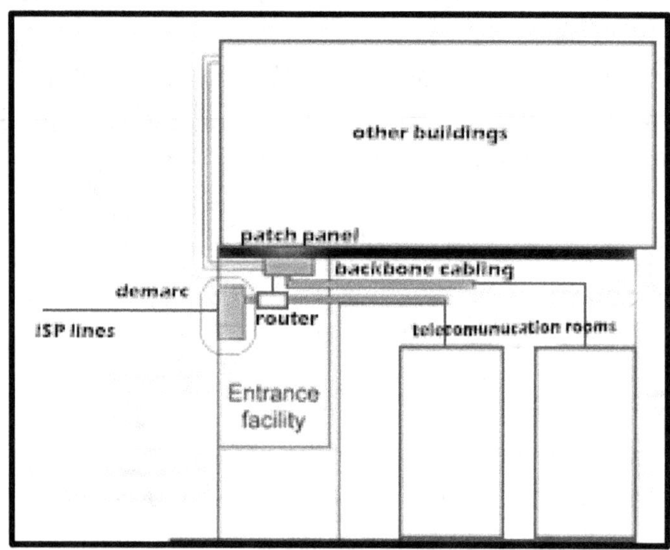

Figure 7.1 The Entrance Facility

2. **Equipment Room**. It refers to the premises that house the network devices or equipment. As shown in Figure 7.2, switches, routers, servers which are inside the network cabinets or racks are normally found in this room. Usually, the cabling from the entrance facility will be routed via a patch panel into the equipment room. It's important to safeguard this room because it contains the servers.

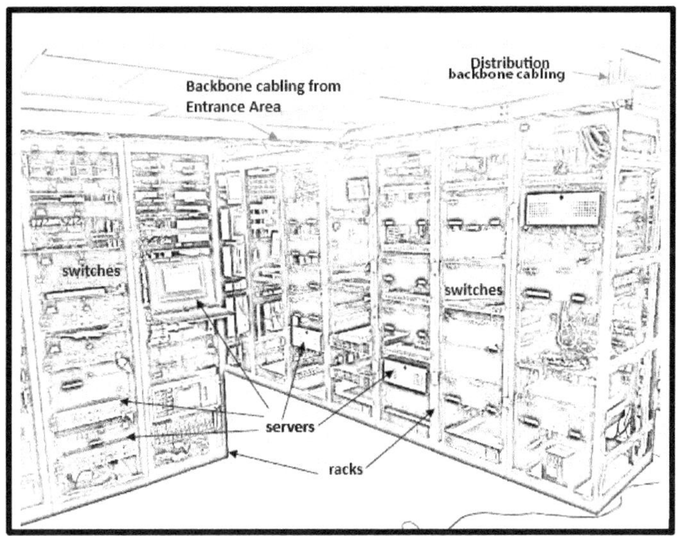

Figure 7.2 The Equipment Room

3. **Backbone Cabling**. It is also called vertical cabling. It connects the telecommunication rooms, the equipment rooms, and the entrance facility. It's typically a twisted pair or fiber optic cable that runs across the building (refer to Figure 7.3).

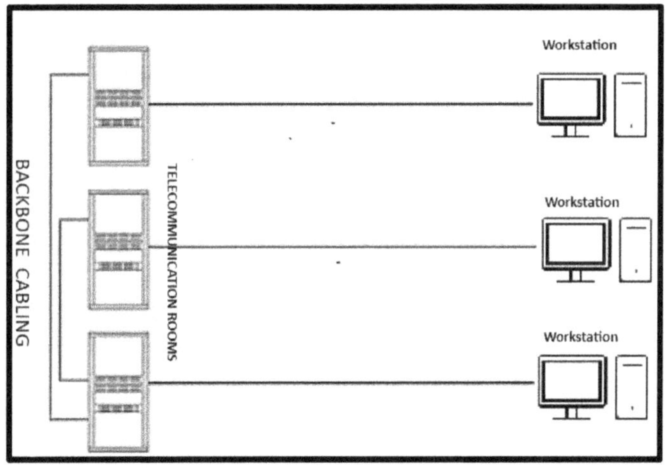

Figure 7.3 The Backbone Cabling

4. **Horizontal Cabling.** Horizontal cabling in a structured cabling system connects the telecommunications room to outlets or the work areas on the premises (refer to Figure 7.3). This cabling is usually an unshielded twisted-pair cable or UTP. Horizontal cabling is like "last mile" cabling before you reach a computer in a work area.

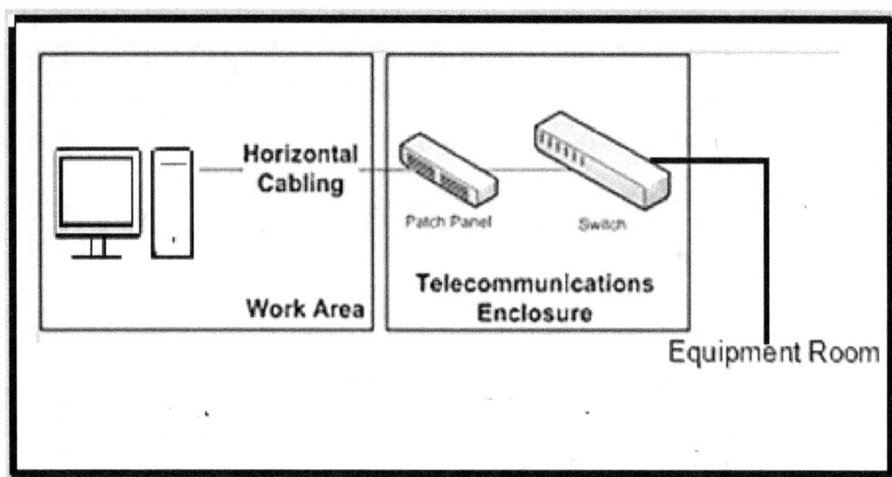

Figure 7.3 Horizontal Cabling

5. **Telecommunications Room**. Telecommunication rooms are special-purpose rooms or enclosures that house telecommunications equipment and wiring (refer to Figure 7.4). Because of the design, scale, and complexity of the equipment and wiring housed in these rooms, they have unique requirements. There should also be one telecommunications room or enclosure per floor of a building.

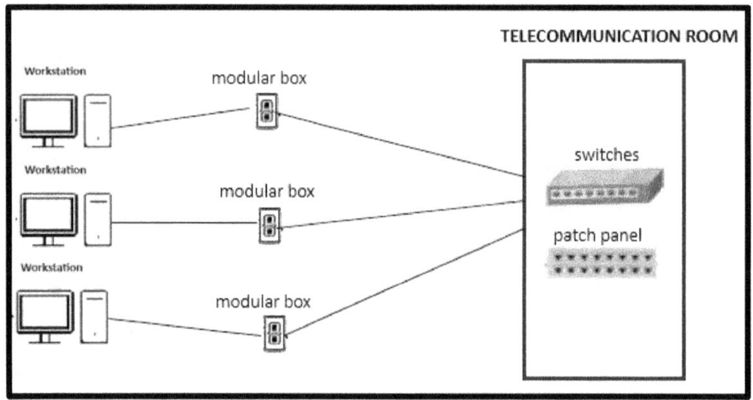

Figure 7.4 Telecommunication Room

6. **Work Area.** The work area is the actual area where an end-user's computer or device is. In this room, there are workstations with various equipment such as laptops, desktop computers, or other Wi-Fi activated devices that plug into a wall socket. Work area components connect the end-user's equipment to the modular boxes in the horizontal cabling subsystem (refer to Figure 7.5).

Figure 7.5 Work Area

To manage our network cabling we need a network cabinet or rack to keep our routers, patch panels, switches, servers, and other networking equipment as well as networking accessories. Another important piece of equipment is a patch panel. It can provide a convenient, neat, and easy-to-manage solution for setting up a cable network that includes multiple wall ports in different rooms and a patch panel can be set up. To cleanly attach network cables from patch panel to our computers we can use modular jack and modular box mounted to our walls. These equipment and accessories can simplify troubleshooting of problems in networks by centralizing cables in one place, which make it easy for network administrators to move, add or change complex network architectures and equipment.

HOW TO WIRE ETHERNET CABLE TO PATCH PANELS AND MODULAR JACK?

It is so simple to wire computers to the server, but it usually creates a large build-up of cables around the server area. It can be managed by connecting the server to the patch panel with the help of short cables, which can also be moved easily when there is a need to. To achieve this kind of wiring, consider the following requirements and steps to wire a patch panel and modular jack:

Materials and Tools Needed

CAT5e or CAT6 cable. This is the basic component to connect end devices to patch panel ports and to connect the ports between two local patch panels.

Copper Patch Panel. A copper patch panel is an installed hardware assembly that includes ports for connecting and managing incoming and outgoing Ethernet cables in a local area network (LAN).

Wire stripper. This tool is used to remove the insulation or protective coating of the network cable. Stripping is the act of removing the protective coating of the network cables in preparation for installation of RJ45 connectors.

LAN Tester. This tool will test whether the wires are set up properly, connected to the appropriate source points, and if the communication strength between the source and destination is strong enough to serve its intended purpose.

Punch down tool. This tool is used to insert wire into insulation-displacement connectors on the punch down IDC blocks of patch panels.

STEPS TO CONFIGURE PATCH PANEL

Step 1: Trim the cable to length. Remove about 1 inch (25mm) of the outer jacket from the end of each cable with the cable stripper.

Step 2: Spread out the 8 cable wires so that you can focus on them separately.

Step 3: Arrange the wires according to the color code indicated in the patch panel and set the wires into the patch panel connectors.

Step 4: Using a punch down tool, firmly press down on each wire until both sets of teeth of the insulation displacement connector grasp it. You may use the cutting edge of the punch down tool to cut the excess wire of Ethernet cables during the pushing operation.

Step 5: Label each cable indicating which room or floor this cable came from.

Step 6: Use a LAN tester to assure that you correctly terminated all the wires.

STEPS TO CONFIGURE RJ45 MODULAR JACK

Step 1: Trim the cable to length. Remove about 1 inch (25mm) of the outer jacket from the end of each cable with the cable stripper.

Step 2: Spread out the 8 cable wires so that you can focus on them separately.

Step 3: Arrange the wires according to the color code indicated in the modular jack and set the wires into the modular jack connectors.

Step 4: Using a punch down tool, firmly press down on each wire until both sets of teeth of the insulation displacement connector grasp it. You may use the cutting edge of the punch down tool to cut the excess wire of Ethernet cables during the pushing operation.

Step 5. Firmly insert the modular jack assembly into the wall plate (modular box) from the back; be sure that the jack's clip is facing up, so that it properly snaps into the wall plate port.

Step 6. Use a LAN tester to test that you correctly terminated all the wires. You may attach a short patch cable from the patch panel's preferred port to the hub or switch nearby. The wire's other end will be connected to a wall socket.

CHAPTER 8

RACEWAY IN CABLING SYSTEM

In this chapter, you will understand the importance of raceways in cabling systems. Once you have a basic understanding of raceways, it will be easier for you to manage your cabling system. After going through this chapter, you are expected to:

1. understand the concept of raceway;
2. demonstrate understanding of the uses and benefits of raceway;
3. discuss, differentiate, and elaborate the different types of raceways; and
4. appreciate the importance of the raceway in cabling system.

C hoosing the right cabling system can have a significant effect on a variety of day-to-day issues in computer networks, such as network performance, data transfer speed, power usage, and even planning strategies. As a result, selecting the proper cabling system is much too critical to be overlooked.

Cable management through raceway configuration is often thought of as simply knowing which cables link to which devices or which racks, they are connected to, but it also entails improving speed, reliability, bandwidth, performance, and lower maintenance thus saving money. It's also a way to make network equipment last longer and save money. failures.

Raceway

Also known as a raceway system. A raceway is essentially any rigid enclosed or semi-enclosed channel that protects, routes, and hides cables and wires. It is usually made of PVC that serves as a physical duct for Ethernet cables that run along the wall. Cables and wires must be secured to function and last to their full capacity. Raceways shield wires and cables from the effects of the environment (heat, humidity, freezing, etc.), corrosion, water damage, and other factors.

Another reason to hide cables is for visual reasons. Raceways are attached to walls or other surfaces, allowing the cables to pass in either direction without interfering with the appeal of the space. Furthermore, as cables are passed through a raceway, no "dust balls" form around them, making the room cleaner not just visually.

BENEFITS OF RACEWAYS

When you need simplified cable management, cable raceways are the way to go. Some of the biggest benefits of raceways include:

1. **Easy to install**: Raceways can be easily installed on any wall in just a few measures. Many cable raceways have adhesive on the backside and can be easily stuck into place.

2. **Simplified cable management**: With raceways, all your cables and wires can be fed through the plastic duct and kept out of sight.

3. **Promotes safety**: Cables and wires that are loose are a safety threat. They can be tripped on or touched by anyone who should not have access to them (like children or pets). Everyone is safer and all cables and wires are secured when cable raceways are used.

4. **Reduced signal interference.** Induction (a process in which an electrical conductor becomes electrified when near a charged body) can cause electromagnetic interference (EMI) when data and power cables are run near together in parallel groups or loops. Data transmission through these lines can be hampered by EMI. To limit the risk of EMI, proper cabling management and the use of raceways can help segment and segregate power and data wires.

5. **Maintenance, troubleshooting, and cabling changes will be easier and have a lower possibility of error.** It's impossible to avoid servicing network equipment, as well as repairing and rerouting cables. Cable management should be provided to facilitate this operation and allow for easy access to minimize downtime or outages.

TYPES OF RACEWAYS

1. **Latching** – This is the most popular and commonly used raceway. It is also known as surface raceways and latching ducts. This raceway has two sides. One side act as a hinge, while the other 'clicks' together to provide the perfect raceway. You open the latch, put some cables inside, then close it back to conceal them from view (refer to Figure 8.1).

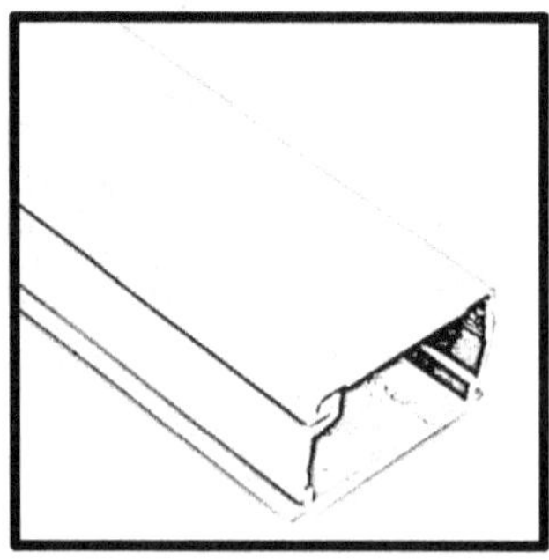

Figure 8.1 Latching Raceway

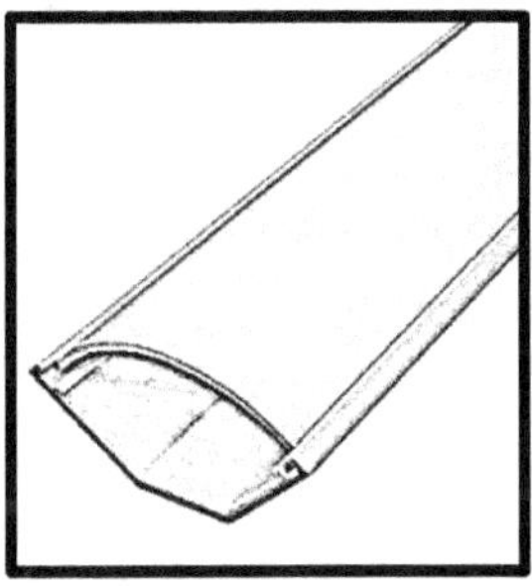

Figure 8.2 Corner Duct Raceway

2.   **Corner Duct** – Corner duct cable raceway has been specially created to provide extra space for cable routing along with the corners of two walls. It conceals external wirings but can be fit into wall corners for a more discreet look.

3. **Overfloor** – If you've ever gone to a conference or a concert where wire is carried across high-traffic floors, you've probably seen one of these. Cables and wires are protected from being tripped over or unplugged by overfloor cable raceways, which run over the floor (refer to Figure 8.3). To minimize generating an unwanted tripping danger, these plastic raceways are usually flatter and lower profile.

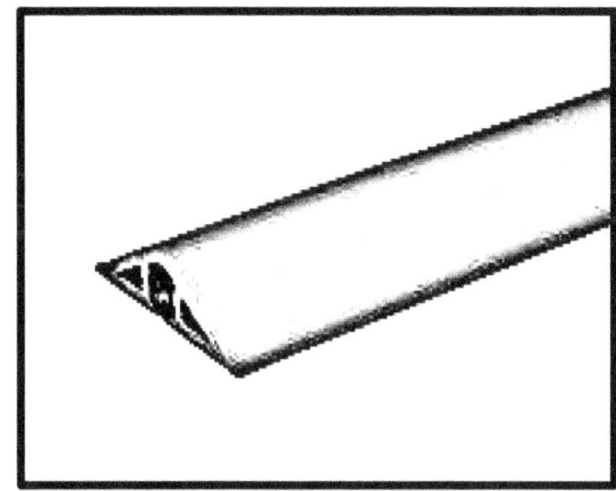

Figure 8.3 Overfloor Raceway

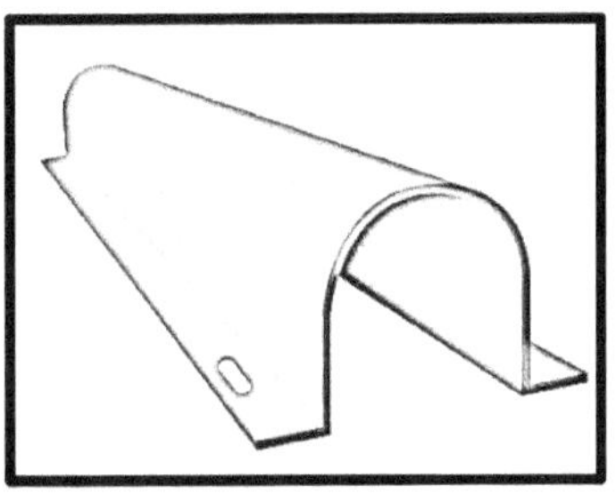

Figure 8.4 Exterior Wire Guards

4. Exterior Wire Guards – Otherwise known as outdoor wire guards, these cable raceways are for use outside to provide means of hiding, concealing, and protecting vertical wiring. They are typically intended to be installed vertically, and they're constructed of high-impact PVC to withstand outdoor elements (refer to Figure 8.4)

5. **Flexible Wire Duct** – These cable raceways are versatile cabling enclosures that can be used in industrial and commercial applications. The flexible material can be protected both horizontally and vertically, and its flexible construction makes it easy to use and mount (refer to Figure 8.5).

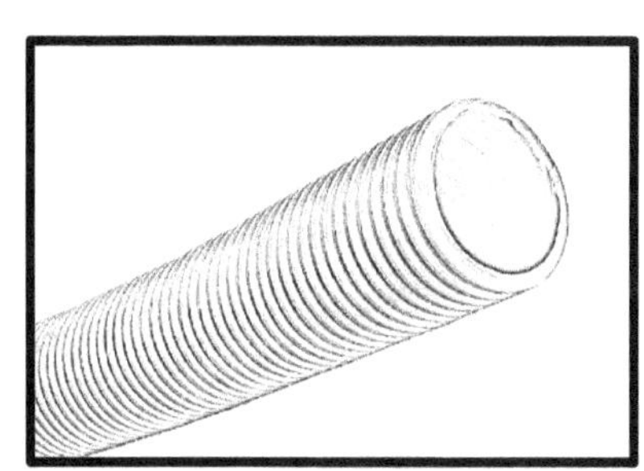

Figure 8.5 Flexible Wire Duct

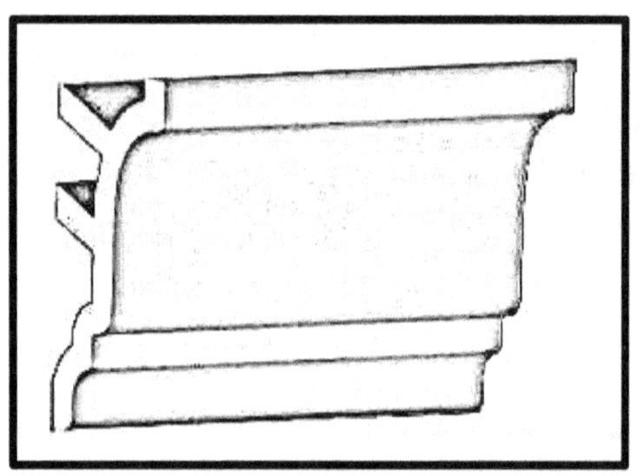

Figure 8.6 Flexible Wire Duct

6. **Crown Raceway.** This raceway is designed to secure and cover low voltage wires, cables, data, voice, and fiber optics. It's simple to place on your wall or ceiling, and it comes with plenty of support in the form of optional cable clamps or other options for maximizing the raceway space. The unique design adds a stylish finish to any room inside your home or office. The raceway comes in white and is resistant (refer to Figure 8.6).

OTHER CABLE SUPPORT EQUIPMENT

1. Bridle rings or cable hooks
2. Cable Retainer
3. Cable clips
4. Cable Tray
5. Cable Routing System

Bridle Rings or Cable Hooks. Bridle rings are popular materials for holding both horizontally and vertically hanging cables. They provide low voltage cable support which comes in easy-to-install types and can support any cable under 600V.

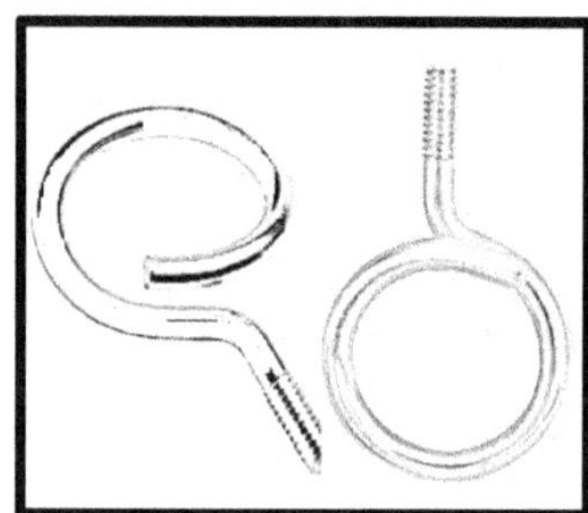

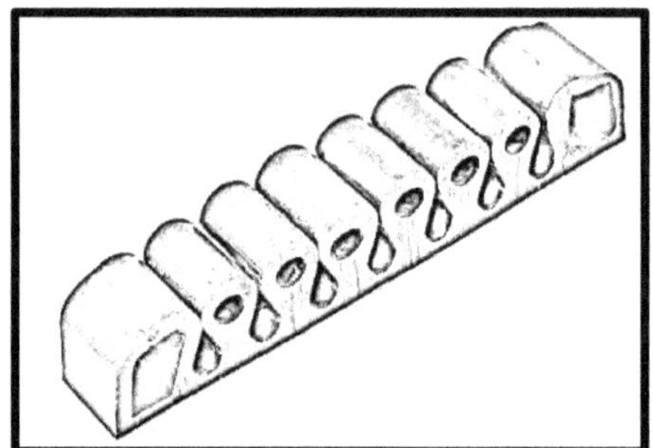

Cable Retainers. Cable retainers are little devices that keep your cable organized, safe, and secure. By keeping the cables tidy, can assist in lessening the danger of trips. caused by loose or trailing cables. As a result, cable retainers are perfect for use at home, in the office, and in the workplace.

Cable Clips. These are a handy way of securing longer runs of cabling and wiring to walls, furniture, along skirting, or behind/around other fittings and fixtures. They're extensively utilized in both the home and the business, as well as everywhere there are lengths of wire flowing between components outside of a cabinet or other container.

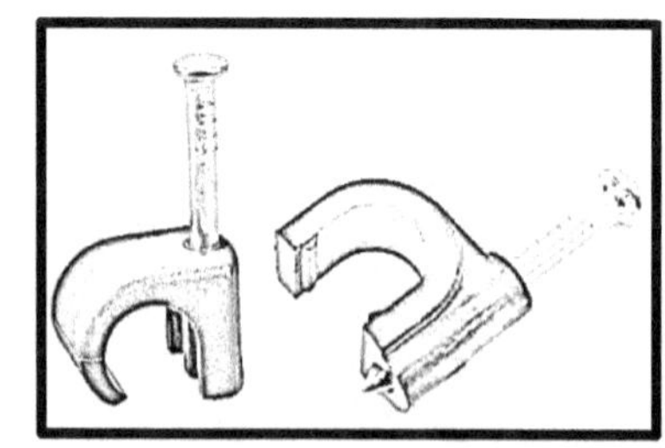

Cable Tray. It's a replacement for open wiring and electrical conduit systems. It supports and protects both power and signal cable, as well as facilitating network upgrades, expansions, reconfigurations, and relocations. It is particularly handy in instances where changes to a wiring system are expected because new cables can be laid easier in the tray rather than pulled through a pipe. It can support high power lines, control cables, twisted pair cables, and fiber optic cables.

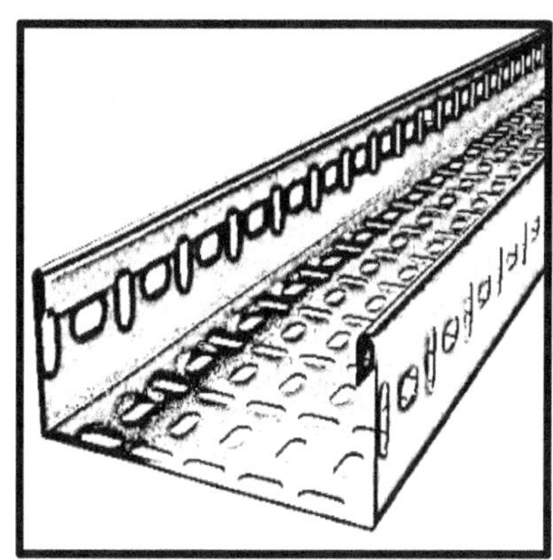

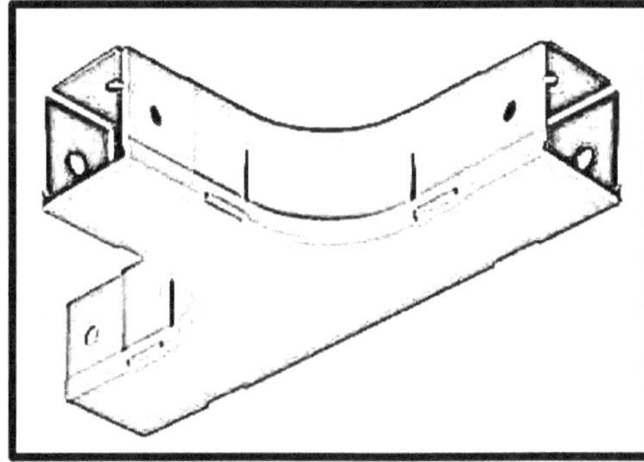

It consists of a set of channels, fittings, and mounting brackets that may be put together to form a structure that protects fiber optic data cables from physical damage that could disrupt or stop signal transmission. It is designed to segregate, route, and protect fiber optic and high-performance copper cabling.

CHAPTER 9

NETWORK SAFETY PRECAUTIONS

In this chapter, you will learn all about safety precautions and their importance in working with a computer network. After going through this module, you are expected to:

1. define Occupational Health and Safety;
2. enumerate and explain personal safety while working with PCs;
3. understand the importance of applying personal safety while working with computer network; and
4. apply Occupational Health and Safety procedures in configuring computer networks.

When working with computers and networks, it's critical to keep safety in mind. Safety precautions in a computer network include the proper safety gear or tools and equipment you need to prepare before doing a job. This means that you should know the personal protective equipment (PPE) you need to have before starting work.

Occupational Health and Safety (OHS)

It refers to rules, policies, procedures, and actions aimed at guaranteeing the health, safety, and well-being of all workers in the workplace. Even though accidents might occur at any time, it is the employer's duty to make sure that precautions are taken to lower the likelihood of accidents and maintain a safe working environment.

Personal Safety in Workplace While Working with Computer

Computers and any hardware devices can be harmful, and if you don't follow the safety requirements when dealing with computers, you or others could be harmed or even killed. There are some precautionary measures to take before working with computers and any hardware devices inside the workplace.

1. **Listen attentively**. Before beginning any activity, pay close attention to your supervisor's instructions to ensure that no accidents or unwelcome events occur in the workplace.

2. **Avoid bringing liquid** such as water inside the workplace. Water is conductive and it will harm any digital device when you accidentally spill water over it.

3. **Be sure to turn off the computer before working on it**. Do not remove any components or internal devices when the computer is turned on.

4. **Always wear personal protective equipment (PPE)**. Your PPE is important because it prepares you for any health and safety risks and gives you extra protection in the event of an accident.

5. **Do not misbehave in the workplace**. When you're inside the room, don't play around. Unnecessary activity in the workplace can cause equipment to be bumped or electric lines to be tripped over.

6. **Practice working safely**. A safe and healthy workplace not only protects you but also your classmates from injury and illness. It can reduce absenteeism and increase productivity and quality of work outputs.

7. **Be Vigilant**. Report fires, accidents, or any broken plugs or exposed electrical wires to your teacher immediately.

Safety Rules While Working with Network Cables

The most crucial consideration while installing network cables is safety. If you follow these steps, you'll have a safe and secure network cable installation:

1. **Always Organized Your Cables**
   - ✓ The performance of the cables will be affected if they are bundled together.
   - ✓ Make sure the unshielded twisted-pair wires that are used to cancel out EMI from outside sources aren't exposed.
   - ✓ Separate the fiber and copper cables in the runs.
   - ✓ Label both ends of the wires, as well as the racks and patch panels.
   - ✓ Cables should not be routed through pipes or holes. Later, you might want to add extra cable runs.

2. **Always Check Your Cables**
   - ✓ Every cable you install and terminate should be tested so you can quickly identify any that may be defective.
   - ✓ Ensure that each horizontal cable you terminate has a port on the patch panel.
   - ✓ Ensure that there are sufficient vertical and horizontal runs, as even disconnecting a single cable can result in downtime.
   - ✓ In the cabling distribution racks, use straight patch panels, while in the cabling distribution area, use angled patch panels.
   - ✓ Route the cables above or below the ports and into the horizontal cable management, rather than across the ports in the patch panels or over other equipment.

    ✓ Make sure the wires and conductors are separated by at least 2 inches (50 mm).
    ✓ Patch cables made of solid-core STP cables with stranded-core RJ-45 connectors should not be used.

3. **Do not twist or staple the cable ties.**
    ✓ Do not apply additional twists or staple the cable ties.
    ✓ Do not pull or stretch the cables beyond their pulling load rate.
    ✓ Do not bend the cables beyond 90°, or their specified bend radius.

4. **Always Maintain Your Cables.** Make sure the cable is free of scratches that might compromise its durability. Don't expose cables to direct sunlight or condensation.

5. **Always Wear your PPE.** Always wear protective clothing when handling cable. There's always the chance of sparks or other electrical hazards. Small copper threads can puncture or harm your skin when you cut the copper cable. Small pieces of cable that break off when they are severed frequently fly into the air. When cutting any form of cable, remember to always use safety glasses. When possible, use gloves and carefully dispose of any waste.

6. **Always Use the Right Tool.** Because each tool is specifically intended for a specific function, using the appropriate tool will also reduce the amount of work required to do a task correctly. For example, using the correct termination tool can increase your productivity by enabling you to install UTP cables faster. Punch down tools improve precision and consistency, resulting in fewer reworks.

Safety Practices when Installing Network Equipment

It is impossible to undermine the importance of adhering to safety protocols. If necessary, measures are not implemented, personnel or the equipment may suffer serious injury. To safeguard your safety and protect the equipment from damage, follow these guidelines. Always be alert and exercise good judgment. Note: Only trained and qualified employees should install any equipment or device.

Use the User's Manual. Only follow the instructions in the User's Manual that came with your device. Otherwise, the device may not function properly.

Keep the work area clean. Keep the working area clear and free before, during, and after installation of computer hardware and network. Avoid wearing loose clothing or jewelry that could be caught in the chassis of computer hardware.

Wear safety glasses. Always wear safety glasses if you're working in any conditions that could be dangerous to your eyes.

Get help lifting heavy objects. Do not attempt to lift an object that is too heavy for you to handle.

Respect electricity. Do not risk electrical shock. Do not perform wiring tasks during electrical storms or operate the router unless it is properly grounded.

Avoid other shock risks. Do not open or remove any hardware device's cover unless instructed. Do not insert objects into openings, avoid spilling liquids, and do not touch exposed wires or terminals.

REFERENCES

Andrea, Harris(2020). *10 Different Types of Networks*. Retrieved April20, 2021, from https://www.networkstraining.com/different-types-of-networks/.

Arsal Jahejo. *Advantages & Disadvantages of Tree Topology*. Retrieved April 16, 2021, from https://computernetworktopology.com/tree-topology/.

Atkins, Jeff (2020, May 14). What is Ethernet Port? Retrieved May 5, 2021, from https://infinity-cable-products.com/blogs/hardware/what-is-an-ethernet-port

Basic Home Network Hardware Components, Devices and Services. Retrieved April 22, 2021, from https://stevessmarthomeguide.com/networking-components/.

Benefits of intranets and extranets. Retrieved April 12, 2021, from https://www.nibusinessinfo.co.uk/content/benefits-extranet.

Biggs, Josh (2023, March 1). *6 Factors When Choosing a Network Topology*. Retrieved April 16, 2021, from https://www.meldium.com/6-factors-when-choosing-a-network-topology/

Bounded or Guided Transmission Media. Retrieved April 27, 2021, from https://www.studytonight.com/computer-networks/bounded-transmission-media#:~:text=Bounded%20or%20Guided%20Transmission%20Media,physical%20limits%20of%20the%20medium

Boyini, Karthikeya (2020, June 19). *Transmission Media*. Retrieved April 4, 2021, from https://www.tutorialspoint.com/Transmission-Media

Category 1 Cable. Retrieved May 5, 2021, from https://www.scribd.com/document/157772991/Category-1-Cable.

Chen, Cheer (2016). Difference Between Straight-Through and Crossover Cable. Retrieved April 17, 2021. https://www.linkedin.com/pulse/difference-between-straight-through-crossover-cable-cheer-chen/

Client Server Architecture in Computer Network. Retrieved April 11, 2021, from https://refugeictsolution.com.ng/2021/05/18/client-server-architecture-in-computer-network/.

Computer Networks: Lecture Notes. Shri Vishnu Engineering College for Women. Vishnu Universal Learning. Retrieved April 4, 2021, from http://www.svecw.edu.in/Docs%5CCSECNLNotes2013.pdf

Computer Networking Notes (2022, April 7). *Network Topologies Explained with Examples*. Retrieved April 16, 2021, from https://www.computernetworkingnotes.com/networking-tutorials/network-topologies-explained-with-examples.html.

Computer Network Types. Java Point. Retrieved April 4, 2021, from https://www.javatpoint.com/types-of-computer-network.

Difference between Internet, Intranet and Extranet. Retrieved April 11, 2021, from https://www.geeksforgeeks.org/difference-between-internet-intranet-and-extranet/.

Differences between Baseband and Broadband Explained. Retrieved April 21, 2021, from https://www.computernetworkingnotes.com/networking-tutorials/differences-between-baseband-and-broadband-explained.html.

Difference of Straight Through and Crossover Cable. Retrieved May 5, 2021, from https://www.cables-solutions.com/difference-between-straight-through-and-crossover-cable.html.

Ethernet Tutorial – Part I: Networking Basics. Retrieved May 3, 2021, from https://www.lantronix.com/resources/networking-tutorials/ethernet-tutorial-networking-basics/.

Goyal, Anshika (2023, March 14). *Types of area networks – LAN, MAN and WAN*. Retrieved May 5, 2021, from https://www.geeksforgeeks.org/types-of-area-networks-lan-man-and-wan/.

Identify Potential Safety Hazards and Implement Proper Safety Procedures Related to Networks. Retrieved June 1, 2021 from https://www.ccexpert.us/operating-systems/identify-potential-safety-hazards-and-implement-proper-safety-procedures-related-to-networks.html

Intranet. Retrieved on April 12, 2021, from https://www.javatpoint.com/intranet.

Introduction to Computers/Networks. Retrieved April 30, 2021, from https://en.wikiversity.org/wiki/Introduction_to_Computers/Networks

Introduction To Communication Technologies. Retrieved April 12, 2021, from https://www.assignmenthelp.net/assignment_help/communication_technologies.

John (2021, September 29). *What Is a Patch Panel and Why Do You Need It?* Retrieved April 20, 2021, from https://community.fs.com/blog/what-is-a-patch-panel-and-why-use-it.html.

Jorgenson, Wyatt. Making a Straight-Through Cable. Retrieved May 6, 2021. From https://www.instructables.com/Making-a-Straight-Through-Cable/

J.T..(2020, August 19). *The Different Types of Network Topologies.* Retrieved April 16, 2021, from https://www.cablewholesale.com/blog/index.php/2020/08/19/the-different-types-of-network-topologies/.

Krishna, Gopal. Unguided Transmission Media. Retrieved April 28, 2021, from https://engineerstutor.com/2018/08/10/unguided-transmission-media-radio-microwave-infrared-satellite/.

Lugo, Alberto. 5 Benefits of having an Intranet. Retrieved April 10, 2021, from https://invidgroup.com/5-benefits-of-having-an-intranet/.

Margaret (2021). What Is Loopback Cable and How to Use It? Retrieved April 21, 2021, from https://community.fs.com/blog/what-is-loopback-cable-and-how-to-use-it.html.

MBA Skool Team (2020, May 25). *WAN - Wide Area Network Meaning & Importance.* Retrieved May 5, 2021, from https://www.mbaskool.com/business-concepts/it-and-systems/13445-wan.html.

Mitchell, Bradley (2021, May 12). What Is an Ethernet Port? Retrieved May 30, 2021, from https://www.lifewire.com/what-is-an-ethernet-port-817546#:~:text=An%20Ethernet%20port%20(also%20called,as%20in%20the%20word%20eat.

Nelson, Charlie(2021). A Guide to Cable Raceways & How to Select the Right One. Retrieved May 17, 2021, from https://www.nelcoproducts.com/blog/cable-raceway/.

Network 101: Peer to Peer Networks. Retrieved April 11, 2021, from http://www.mindpride.net/root/Extras/peer_to_peer_networking.htm.

Network Architecture. Tiered & Peer to Peer. Retrieved April 10, 2021, from https://study.com/academy/lesson/network-architecture-tiered-peer-to-peer.html.

Network Cable Crimping and Testing Tools. Retrieved April 19, 2021, from https://www.computernetworkingnotes.com/networking-tutorials/network-cable-crimping-and-testing-tools.html.

Network Cable Installation Guidelines (2019, August 4). Retrieved June 1, 2021, from https://mscelectrical.com/network-cable-installations/

Network Devices Explained. Retrieved April 21, 2021, from https://blog.netwrix.com/2019/01/08/network-devices-explained/.

Network Tools and Their Purpose. Retrieved April 22, 2021, from https://www.cmple.com/learn/network-tools-and-their-purpose.

Pabello, Shirley. Tools, Materials and Equipment for Networking. Retrieved April 21, 2021, from https://www.slideshare.net/shierlypabello/tools-materials-and-equipment-for-networking.

Peer to Peer vs. Client-Server Networks. Retrieved April 11, 2021, from https://onlinecomputertips.com/support-categories/networking/673-peer-to-peer-vs-client-server-networks/.

Petryschuk, Steve (2021, February 3). *11 Types of Networks: Understanding the Differences.* Retrieved April 12, 2021, from https://www.auvik.com/franklyit/blog/types-of-networks/

Razo, Jaya (2018). Technical Description: Modulator Demodulator (Modem). Retrieved April 21, 2021, from https://salirickandres.altervista.org/technical-description-modulator-demodulator-modem/.

Refuge_2020 (2021, June 14). *Hybrid Network Architecture.* Retrieved April 16, 2022, from http://refugeictsolution.com.ng/2021/06/14/hybrid-network/.

Rhee, Ed (2011, August 4). How to make your own Ethernet cable. Retrieved May 6, 2021, from https://www.cnet.com/how-to/how-to-make-your-own-ethernet-cable/

Schultz, Don (Sep 09, 2021). T568a vs T568b: Which to Use. Retrieved May 5, 2021, from https://www.truecable.com/blogs/cable-academy/t568a-vs-t568b.

Singh, Cadell (2018, January 13). Types of Network Architecture. Retrieved April 10, 2021, from https://dev.to/cadellsinghh_25/types-of-network-architecture-56i7

Singh, Chaitanya. Computer Network Topology – Mesh, Star, Bus, Ring and Hybrid. Retrieved April 16, 2021, from https://beginnersbook.com/2019/03/computer-network-topology-mesh-star-bus-ring-and-hybrid/

The Wrong Things to Do. Retrieved June 1, 2021, from https://ict123.wordpress.com/topics/safety-rules-and-regulation/the-wrong-things-to-do.

Touhid (2020, November 28). *What is Networking of Computer?* Retrieved May 2, 2021, from https://cyberthreatportal.com/what-is-networking-of-computer/.

Tyari, Paper (2023). *Network Topologies.* Retrieved April 15, 2021, from https://www.papertyari.com/general-awareness/it-knowledge/network-topologies/.

What is an extranet? Retrieved April 12, 2021, from https://teaching.shu.ac.uk/aces/ict/de/what_is_%20extranet.htm.

What are Ethernet Crossover Cables? Retrieved May 4, 2021, from
https://www.computercablestore.com/what-are-ethernet-crossover-cables

What Is an Ethernet Cable? Retrieved May 4, 2021, from
https://www.firefold.com/blogs/news/what-is-an-ethernet-cable.

What is Network Architecture. Retrieved April 10, 2021, from
https://www.cisco.com/c/en/us/solutions/enterprise-networks/what-is-network-architecture.html.

What is a Network Bridge? Retrieved April 20, 2021, from
https://networkinterview.com/?s=bridge.

What Is the Difference Between a Wi-Fi Extender and a Wi-Fi Repeater? (2021, January 25). Retrieved April 21, 2022, from
https://www.hellotech.com/blog/difference-between-wifi-extender-and-wifi-repeater.

What Is Structured Cabling and Why Use It? (2018, October 9). Retrieved May 13, 2021, from http://www.fiber-optic-transceiver-module.com/what-is-structured-cabling.html

Wildpigsuperza (2013,November 16). Local Area Network (LAN). Retrieved May 2, 202, from https://wildpigsuperza.wordpress.com/2013/11/16/local-area-network-lan/.

Winkelman, Roy (2013). *Topology*. Retrieved on April 16, 2021, from
https://fcit.usf.edu/network/chap5/chap5.htm

Yong, Kak (2012, April 17). Network Communication Technology. Retrieved April 11, 2021, from https://www.slideshare.net/makyong1/chapter-34-12573637

Yong, Kak (2012, April 17). Wireless Transmission Media. Retrieved April 29, 2021, from https://www.slideshare.net/makyong1/wireless-transmission-media

Zhu, Aria (2016). How to Use Punch Down Tool? Retrieved April 21, 201, from
https://medium.com/@AriaZhu/how-to-use-punch-down-tool-98ded43a00e7.

9 786214 708963